WILLIAMS-SONOMA

AMERICAN
CHRISTMAS

WILLIAMS-SONOMA

AMERICAN
CHRISTMAS

GENERAL EDITOR
Chuck Williams

RECIPES
Brigit Binns, Kerri Conan, Abigail Dodge,
Jean Galton, Lori Longbotham, Tina Salter

TEXT
Judith H. Dern, Steve Siegelman

PHOTOGRAPHY
Jim Franco

STYLING
Sara Slavin

FOOD STYLING
Kevin Crafts

Oxmoor House®

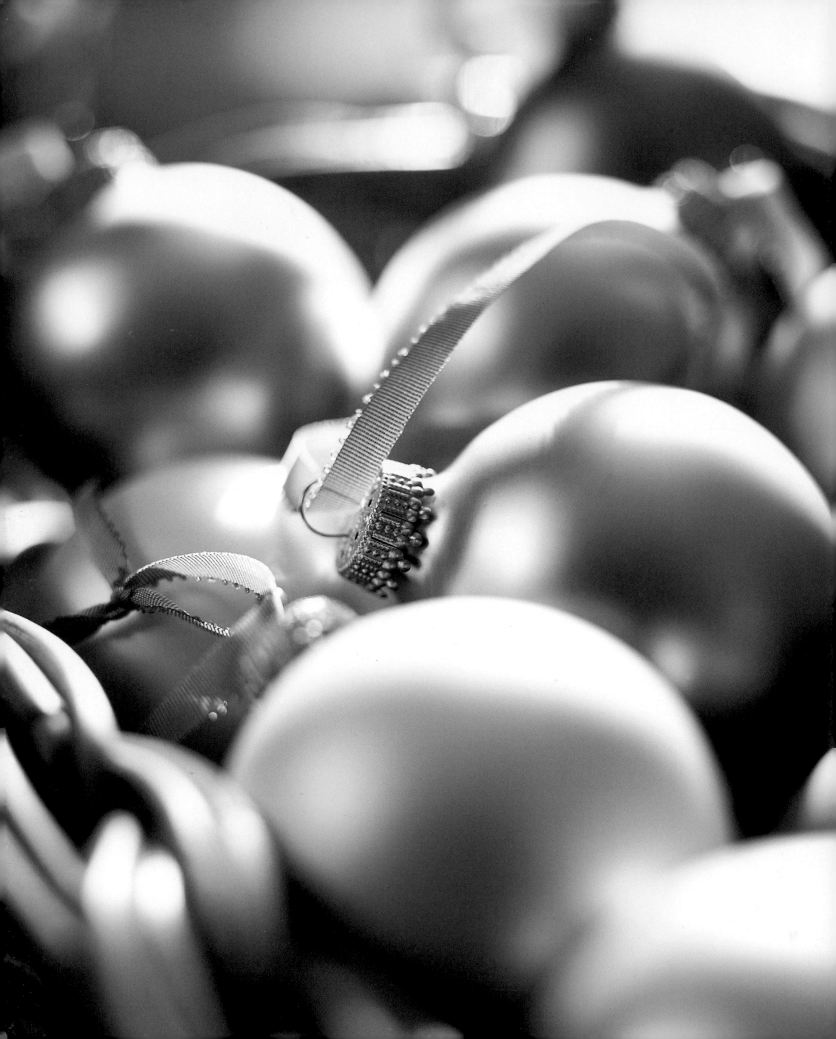

60

126

CONTENTS

*At Christmas play
and make good cheer,
For Christmas comes
but once a year.*

The Farmer's Daily Diet
Thomas Tusser (c. 1524–80)

INTRODUCTION

Every winter, all across America, the arrival of the Christmas season invites us to step out of our hectic lives and share the joy of timeless holiday traditions with family and friends. Trimming the tree, decorating the house, exchanging handmade treats and home-baked cookies, feasting beside a roaring fire, hosting a holiday open house, giggling with children over a mug of eggnog—these are the once-a-year rituals that make the season so enchanting and memorable.

With a little planning, making those moments a part of your Christmas does not have to be difficult or even time-consuming. In these pages, you'll find dozens of easy, celebratory recipes, creative decorating and gift-giving inspirations, simple tips, and visual "idea-starters" for holiday entertaining—all designed for real people with busy lives. They are organized into eight festive occasions, with menus and step-by-step work plans to help you stay on schedule. Ideally, you will be inspired to mix and match ideas and recipes, and to throw in some family favorites of your own.

From New England to California, the pleasures of Christmas are a happy blending of old-world customs and fresh, imaginative ideas. In that spirt, this book is designed to rekindle many beloved traditions—and spark a few new ones—in your corner of America. The personal touches that you bring to Christmas year after year add up to something truly special. Because no matter how grand or simple, a tradition is a memory in the making, a symbol of love that one generation gives to the next. And when all the presents have been unwrapped, that memory remains the greatest Christmas gift of all.

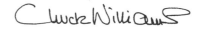

TREE-TRIMMING TOAST

Christmastime begins the day the tree comes home, the boxes of ornaments are unpacked, and the house is filled with the scent of pine. Make the most of that happy moment with a party that brings family, friends, and neighbors together to trim the tree and toast the start of the holiday season. It is an event with something for everyone, even the host: kids and adults enjoy having a hand in the tree's magical transformation, and you end up with a beautifully decorated tree and a lot of happy memories.

Much of the easy finger-food menu can be made in advance, so the host can enjoy the party too. String the tree with lights before the guests arrive to make the trimming easier. Miniature white lights make a sparkling background for homemade ribbon ornaments and paper chains, augmented with store-bought decorations in reds and golds. Arrange the ornaments in baskets, and set out the food on platters around the room, with Champagne and drinks on a side table to keep traffic flowing smoothly. As afternoon turns to dusk, and the trimming winds down, serve dessert by the fire.

MENU

Christmas Bubbly

Spiced Pumpkin Seeds

Blue Cheese Celery

Savory Herb Shortbread

Deviled Red Potatoes

*Rissoles Filled with Shaved
Beef and Horseradish Cream*

Potted Toffee Puddings

PLANNING AHEAD

2 DAYS AHEAD
Mix blue cheese filling

Make shortbread

Roast pumpkin seeds

1 DAY AHEAD
Chill sparkling wine and juice

Trim celery

Roast red potato shells

Make filling for red potatoes

Thaw filo dough

Prepare beef filling for rissoles

2 HOURS AHEAD
Assemble red potatoes

Fill rissoles

Bake toffee puddings

JUST BEFORE SERVING
Bake rissoles

Top toffee puddings

Ribbon Ornaments

RIBBON • ORNAMENT HANGERS

Create a simple design, such as a geometric shape
or a flower, and use it for making ribbon ornaments.
The ornament shown here is a variation on the
old-fashioned paper chain.

ONE Gather brightly colored ribbons that complement
the palette of your tree. Use wider ribbon for larger
ornaments and narrow ribbon for smaller ones.

TWO Sketch a design, using pencil and drawing paper.
Using the drawing, measure the length of ribbon needed
for each segment and cut ribbon strips as needed.

THREE Affix a spot of glue onto one end of a strip, loop
the strip, and press to seal. Repeat with the remaining
strips, assembling the ornament to match your design.
Attach a hanger to the top loop, or slip the top loop
directly onto the tree branch.

Christmas Bubbly

This holly-red cocktail is easy to make, one flute at a time, as the guests arrive. In addition to Champagne, keep some sparkling grape juice on ice, so you can offer an alcohol-free option. When all the guests are assembled, raise a glass to toast the season and thank everyone for their company—and decorating help.

¾ cup pomegranate syrup

9 bottles sparkling wine or sparkling grape juice, or a combination

Pour 1 teaspoon pomegranate syrup in the bottom of each Champagne flute. Slowly fill with ¾ cup sparkling wine. For a version without alcohol, use sparkling grape juice. Serve immediately.

MAKES ABOUT 36 SERVINGS

Spiced Pumpkin Seeds

Place small bowls of these full-flavored, deep green seeds around the room. Known as pepitas, *pumpkin seeds are widely used in Mexican cooking to thicken sauces and to garnish salads and desserts.*

6 cups raw hulled pumpkin seeds

2 tablespoons olive oil

¼ cup firmly packed turbinado sugar or golden brown sugar

1 tablespoon cumin seeds

Sea salt

2 cinnamon sticks, broken into small pieces

½ nutmeg seed

¼ teaspoon cayenne pepper

Preheat oven to 350°F. Line 2 large, rimmed baking sheets with parchment paper (or toast the seeds on 1 pan in 2 batches).

Put the pumpkin seeds in a large bowl and pick through and discard any that are broken or discolored. Drizzle with the olive oil and toss to coat evenly.

In a spice grinder, combine the sugar, cumin seeds, 2 teaspoons salt, cinnamon sticks, nutmeg, and cayenne and grind to a fine powder. Sprinkle over the pumpkin seeds and toss until coated. Spread half of the mixture onto each prepared baking sheet. Bake, stirring frequently with a metal spatula for even browning, until the popping of the seeds subsides, about 15 minutes.

Remove from oven and let cool completely on the pans, stirring occasionally. The color of the seeds will deepen. Store in an airtight container for up to 2 days.

MAKES 6 CUPS, OR 12 SERVINGS

Blue Cheese Celery

Select a creamy blue cheese, such as Gorgonzola, bleu d'Auvergne, or Maytag, for these crisp, hazelnut-laced celery hors d'oeuvres. You can make the filling up to 2 days in advance, and trim the celery the night before.

Preheat oven to 350°F. Spread the nuts on a rimmed baking sheet and toast, shaking the sheet twice to brown evenly, 5–7 minutes. Transfer the hot nuts to a kitchen towel and rub vigorously to remove the skins. When cool, store the nuts in an airtight container.

In a food processor, or in a bowl and using a small fork, mix together the cheeses and ¼ cup buttermilk, adding more buttermilk as needed to achieve a smooth consistency. Mix in the sage and season lightly with salt and pepper. Cover tightly with plastic wrap and refrigerate for up to 2 days.

The night before the party, slice each celery stalk on the diagonal into 1½-inch pieces. Cut a thin slice from the curved back of each piece so it will lie flat. Trim the hearts and leaves for garnish. Place the celery and garnish in ice water in the refrigerator.

To assemble, drain the celery and let air-dry. Finely chop the nuts and add to the cheese mixture. Taste and adjust the seasoning. Spoon about 1 tablespoon of the mixture into each celery hollow. Cover and refrigerate for up to 2 hours before serving.

MAKES ABOUT 4 DOZEN PIECES, OR 12 SERVINGS

¾ cup whole hazelnuts

¾ lb blue cheese, at room temperature, crumbled

6 oz cream cheese, at room temperature

¼ cup buttermilk, plus more if needed

½ cup loosely packed fresh sage leaves, finely minced

Coarse salt and freshly ground pepper

12 celery stalks, about 6 inches each, plus tender celery hearts with leaves intact

Savory Herb Shortbread

Prepare this simple recipe up to a week in advance. As the dough rests, the butter absorbs the flavor of the minced herbs and softens their texture. Serve these rich and buttery "cookies" on festive plates.

Combine the butter and cheese in a large bowl. On a cutting board, chop together the thyme, oregano, and rosemary leaves as finely as possible. Add to the butter mixture and mash with a fork until evenly distributed. Add the flour and the 1 teaspoon salt. Mix first with the fork and then with your hands until the flour is incorporated.

Divide the dough in half and quickly roll each portion into a log 8 inches long by 1½ inches in diameter. Wrap each log in plastic wrap and refrigerate for at least 24 hours or up to 3 days, or freeze for up to 1 week. (If frozen, thaw in the refrigerator for 24–36 hours before slicing.)

Preheat oven to 350°F. Line 2 rimmed baking sheets with parchment paper. Cut each log into slices ¼ inch thick. Place on the prepared sheets, spacing about 1 inch apart.

Bake until the edges begin to brown, 12–15 minutes. Remove from oven, sprinkle lightly with additional sea salt, if using, and let cool for 2–3 minutes on the baking sheets, then transfer to wire racks to cool completely. Store in airtight containers between layers of parchment paper for up to 2 days.

MAKES ABOUT 5 DOZEN SHORTBREADS, OR 12 SERVINGS

1 cup unsalted butter, at room temperature, cut into small cubes

1 cup finely shredded sharp cheddar cheese

Leaves from 1 small bunch fresh thyme

Leaves from 1 small bunch fresh oregano

Leaves from 2 or 3 fresh rosemary sprigs

2 cups all-purpose flour

1 teaspoon sea salt, plus more for garnish (optional)

Deviled Red Potatoes

24 small red potatoes, 4–5 lb total weight

¼ cup olive oil

8 hard-boiled large eggs

¾ lb thick-cut bacon, about 10 slices, fried crisp, drained on paper towels, and crumbled

1 red bell pepper, seeded and minced

8 green onions, white parts and 2 inches of the greens, minced

1 cup mayonnaise

½ cup sour cream

2 tablespoons Dijon mustard

Coarse salt and freshly ground white pepper

Paprika, for garnish

Crisply roasted red potato shells hold a devilishly rich egg-and-potato salad studded with bacon and dusted with paprika. The filling benefits from advance preparation, which allows time for the flavors to blend. Spoon it into the shells no more than 2 hours before serving.

Preheat oven to 350°F.

Spread the potatoes in a large, shallow roasting pan or on a rimmed baking sheet. Drizzle with the olive oil and brush or rub to coat thoroughly. Roast, shaking the pan once or twice during cooking, until the largest potato is tender when pierced with a skewer, 30–40 minutes. Set aside to cool completely. Leave oven set at 350°F.

Meanwhile, peel the eggs and separate the whites from the yolks. Put the yolks in a bowl and set aside. Place a coarse-mesh sieve or potato ricer over a large bowl and push the egg whites through. Set aside.

When the potatoes are completely cool, cut each potato in half crosswise. Using a melon baller or sharp spoon, gently scoop out the potato flesh onto a large cutting board, leaving a shell ¼ inch thick. Coarsely chop the potato flesh and add it to the bowl holding the egg whites. Add the bacon, bell pepper, and green onions and toss gently.

Return the potato shells, cut side down, to the roasting pan. Roast for 10 minutes, then turn cut side up and roast until golden, about 10 minutes longer. Let cool completely on wire racks until crisp and firm. Gently stack the cooled shells, cover, and refrigerate for up to 24 hours.

While the potato shells are roasting, mash the egg yolks with a fork. Whisk in the mayonnaise, sour cream, mustard, 1½ teaspoons salt, and 1 teaspoon white pepper until smooth and creamy. Pour the dressing over the potato mixture and toss gently to coat. Cover tightly with plastic wrap and refrigerate for up to 24 hours.

To assemble, stir the potato mixture and taste and adjust the seasoning. Fill the potato shells and arrange them on a serving platter. Serve immediately, or cover and refrigerate for up to 2 hours. Just before serving, dust the tops with paprika.

MAKES 4 DOZEN PIECES, OR 12 SERVINGS

Rissoles Filled with Shaved Beef and Horseradish Cream

Rissoles, small, deep-fried puff pastry or brioche turnovers that conceal a savory filling, are traditionally served at Christmastime in many French homes. This baked filo version is lighter than its French counterpart.

To make the filling, preheat oven to 400°F. Rinse the beef and pat dry with paper towels. Rub with 1 teaspoon salt and ½ teaspoon pepper. Let stand at room temperature for about 30 minutes.

Place a large, heavy ovenproof frying pan (preferably cast iron) over medium-high heat until very hot. Add the olive oil and as soon as it starts to smoke, add the beef. Sear the first side, without moving the beef, until a crust forms, 4–5 minutes. Flip and sear the other side the same way. Transfer the pan to the oven and roast until medium-rare and an instant-read thermometer reads 135°F, about 15 minutes. Transfer the beef to a deep plate to collect its juices and cover loosely with aluminum foil.

While the beef is resting, make the sauce. In a small frying pan over medium heat, melt the butter until foaming. Add the horseradish and sauté, stirring constantly, until fragrant and softened, about 3 minutes. Stir in the accumulated beef juices and reduce until almost dry. Add the cream and cook until it starts to bubble, then reduce the heat to low and simmer until thick enough to coat the back of a spoon, 10–15 minutes. Stir in the parsley and remove from the heat. When cool, cover both the beef and sauce tightly and refrigerate for at least 4 or up to 24 hours.

When ready to make the rissoles, "shave" the cold beef by cutting paper-thin slices against the grain. In a bowl, toss the shaved beef with just enough of the sauce to moisten. Taste and adjust the seasoning. You should have about 3 cups filling.

Line a rimmed baking sheet with parchment paper. Unwrap the filo sheets and cover the stack with a damp kitchen towel. You will need about 12 sheets; leftover sheets can be tightly wrapped in plastic wrap and refrigerated for up to 2 days or refrozen. Remove 1 filo sheet from the stack, keeping the unused sheets covered with the towel. Lightly brush the sheet with olive oil, then, using a pastry wheel, cut it in half lengthwise and then in half crosswise, to make 4 rectangles. Sprinkle each sheet (4 rectangles) with 1 tablespoon of the bread crumbs.

With a narrow end facing you, place about 1 tablespoon of the filling 1 inch from the nearest edge. Fold the end over to cover the filling, fold in the sides, and then roll up into a cylinder about 2 inches long. Brush the ends and top of the rissole with oil and place it on a prepared baking sheet. Repeat until all the filling is used, arranging the rissoles, not touching, in a single layer. When the pan is full, cover the rissoles with a sheet of parchment, and stack the remainder on top. Cover with plastic wrap and refrigerate for 1–2 hours.

When ready to bake, preheat oven to 375°F. Line 2 rimmed baking sheets with parchment paper and fit each with a wire rack. Place the rissoles about 1 inch apart on prepared baking sheets. Bake until evenly golden brown, 10–15 minutes. Let cool for 5 minutes, then serve.

MAKES ABOUT 4 DOZEN RISSOLES, OR 12 SERVINGS

FILLING

1 top round of beef, London broil cut, 1½–2 lb

Coarse salt and freshly ground pepper

1 tablespoon olive oil

1 tablespoon unsalted butter

¼ cup grated horseradish root or 2 tablespoons prepared horseradish, plus more to taste

1 cup heavy cream

½ cup finely chopped fresh flat-leaf parsley

PASTRY

1 package (1 lb) filo dough, about 20 sheets, thawed in the refrigerator for 24–36 hours

1 cup olive oil, for brushing

About 1 cup plain dried bread crumbs

Potted Toffee Puddings

The visible signature of a toffee topping is a rich crackling surface. These small pudding cakes can be baked in the morning while the syrup bubbles away on the stove top. Then, at party time, top the pots with the syrup and pass them briefly under the broiler.

Preheat oven to 325°F. Grease twelve 1-cup flameproof ramekins and place in a deep roasting pan.

Put the dates in a small saucepan over medium-high heat and add 1 cup water. Bring just to a boil, then immediately remove from the heat and stir in the baking soda. Set aside to cool for about 30 minutes, stirring occasionally. The mixture will be thick and glossy, with some date pieces remaining. Bring a full kettle of water to a boil.

Meanwhile, in a bowl, sift together the flour, baking powder, and salt. In a large bowl, using a stand mixer fitted with the paddle attachment, or using a handheld mixer, cream the butter on medium speed until fluffy, about 3 minutes. Add the brown and granulated sugars and beat until light and the sugars are dissolved, 2–3 minutes. Scrape down the sides of the bowl. Reduce the mixer speed to medium-low and add the eggs, one at a time, beating well after each addition and scraping down the bowl.

Reduce the mixer speed to low and beat in the flour mixture in 3 batches, alternating with the date mixture in 3 batches. Scrape down the bowl after each addition and be careful not to overmix. Divide the batter evenly among the ramekins (about ½ cup batter in each). With the back of a spoon, gently smooth the tops, forming a slight indentation in the center and pushing the batter to the edges.

Pour boiling water into the roasting pan to reach a little more than halfway up the sides of the ramekins. Bake until a toothpick inserted in the center of a pudding comes out clean, about 30 minutes. Immediately remove the ramekins from the water bath and transfer to wire racks to cool. Leave at room temperature, covered with a dry towel.

To make the toffee syrup, in a saucepan over medium heat, combine the butter, brown sugar, half-and-half, and cream, stirring to melt the butter and dissolve the sugar. Bring to a simmer and let bubble gently without boiling, whisking frequently, until the syrup is thick and coats the back of a spoon, 15–20 minutes. Remove from the heat, stir in the vanilla and salt, and set aside. When cool, cover tightly and refrigerate until needed. You should have about 2 cups.

Before serving, preheat broiler and position the rack 4 inches from the heat source. Arrange the ramekins on a rimmed baking sheet, and spoon 2 tablespoons syrup on top of each pudding. Broil, watching constantly, until the syrup bubbles and caramelizes, about 2 minutes. Alternatively, use a kitchen torch to caramelize the syrup. Serve when cool enough to handle. Pass the remaining syrup in a small pitcher.

MAKES 12 INDIVIDUAL PUDDINGS

16 Medjool dates, about ½ lb total weight, pitted and coarsely chopped

1½ teaspoons baking soda

2½ cups all-purpose flour

1½ teaspoons baking powder

½ teaspoon coarse salt

¾ cup unsalted butter, at room temperature

½ cup firmly packed golden brown sugar

½ cup granulated sugar

6 large eggs, at room temperature

TOFFEE SYRUP

2 tablespoons unsalted butter

1½ cups firmly packed brown sugar

1 cup half-and-half

1 cup heavy cream

½ teaspoon vanilla extract

Pinch of coarse salt

NEW ENGLAND COOKIE EXCHANGE

More than a century ago, New Englanders came up with this practical way to share the pleasures, and the work, of holiday baking. Today, the cookie exchange has become a beloved American Christmas tradition and a perfect occasion for holiday entertaining.

Invite guests to bring three or four dozen Christmas cookies. (Although that may sound like a lot, it is usually only one or two batches.) Encourage them to bake family favorites, and collect the recipes from them a week ahead of time so you can make copies to distribute. As the party approaches, bake additional cookies using the recipes in this chapter for inspiration. The Lemon Cookies with Wintry Decorations (page 35) can be left unfrosted for your friends to decorate at the party.

Set up a table with cookie-friendly beverages, such as milk, hot spiced cider, and cocoa. As guests arrive, arrange their cookies on platters for sampling and exchanging. Provide cookie jars decorated with ribbon and a fan of recipe cards so everyone can assemble his or her own assortment to take home.

PLANNING AHEAD

2–3 WEEKS AHEAD
Send out cookie exchange invitations

1 WEEK AHEAD
Collect recipes from guests
Gather jars, ribbon, labels, and cards

1 DAY AHEAD
Write out recipe cards
Decorate cookie jars
Bake cookies

1 HOUR AHEAD
Make cocoa, hot cider
Set coffee table for party
Chill pitcher of milk

JUST BEFORE SERVING
Reheat the cocoa, cider

GING   CRIS

1²/₃ cups all purpose

1 teaspoon ground

3/4 teaspoon ground

pinch of ground n

1/2 teaspoon baki

1/4 teaspoon sal

1/2 cup unsalte

Cookie Jars

GLASS JARS • CARDS • RIBBON • LABELS • COLORED PEN

At the party, present each guest with a big, pretty glass jar, complete with recipe booklet, for filling with a mix of cookies—flat ones on the bottom, more delicate iced or jam-filled ones on top—brought by other guests.

ONE Select clear glass jars that are tall and wide enough to hold all the different cookie varieties. Buy prepunched cards, or cut out cards from card stock and punch a hole in the top.

TWO Affix a label on the top of each card. Using a pen with colorful ink, write the name of the cookie on the label and the recipe on the card, making one card per cookie recipe per guest (or use your computer to print out the recipes).

THREE Thread a short length of ribbon through each complete set of cards, tie securely, and then use a second piece of ribbon to tie the cards to the jar lid.

Lemon Cookies with Wintry Decorations

These rich buttery cookies make perfect small canvases for decoration. If you like, use a thin straw to punch a hole in the dough before baking, then attach a string to the finished cookie to hang it as an ornament.

Preheat oven to 350°F. Lightly grease 2 baking sheets or line them with parchment paper.

In a large bowl, using an electric mixer on medium speed, beat the butter, granulated sugar, lemon zest, and salt until light and fluffy. Add the egg yolk and lemon juice and beat until blended. Reduce the mixer speed to low and gradually beat in the flour just until blended and the dough comes together.

Turn out the dough onto a work surface. Divide the dough in half, then gather up each portion and press into a disk. Wrap 1 disk in plastic wrap and set aside. (If the dough is soft, wrap both disks in plastic wrap and refrigerate until firm, about 30 minutes.)

Sprinkle the work surface with flour. Place the unwrapped disk on the floured surface, and sprinkle the top of the dough with a little flour. Roll out the dough ¼ inch thick, sprinkling more flour under and over the dough as needed to prevent sticking.

Using a 2½-inch round or decorative cookie cutter, cut out as many cookies as possible, cutting them close together. Pull away the scraps of dough from around the shapes and set the scraps aside. Using an offset spatula, carefully transfer the cookies to the prepared baking sheets, spacing them about ¾ inch apart. Gather up the reserved dough scraps and gently press them into a disk. Repeat the rolling and cutting process with the scraps and then with the second dough disk.

Bake the cookies until lightly browned around the edges, about 12 minutes. Let the cookies cool on the baking sheets on wire racks for 5 minutes, then transfer the cookies to the racks to cool completely before decorating.

To make the icing, in a large bowl, using the mixer on medium speed, combine the meringue powder and 6 tablespoons warm water. Reduce the mixer speed to low and gradually beat in the confectioners' sugar until blended, then beat on high speed until thick and smooth, about 5 minutes. Beat in more warm water, 1 tablespoon at a time, if the icing is too thick to spread or pipe. Scrape down the sides of the bowl and cover the surface with a damp paper towel if not using immediately. If you are coloring the icing, divide it among small bowls, one for each color. Add a drop or so of coloring to each bowl and stir until blended. Repeat as needed to create the desired color.

To decorate the cookies, using a pastry bag fitted with a narrow tip, outline the edges of a cookie with some of the icing, then use a small, damp pastry brush to spread an even layer of icing within the border. (If the icing is too thick, add a drop of warm water and stir until blended.) Alternatively, use the pastry bag to pipe designs on the cookies. Let the icing set completely. While the icing is still soft, decorate the cookies with colored sugars, sprinkles, or other decorations as desired. Let set completely.

MAKES ABOUT 3 DOZEN COOKIES

1 cup unsalted butter, at room temperature

1 cup granulated sugar

1 teaspoon grated lemon zest

¼ teaspoon salt

1 large egg yolk

1 tablespoon fresh lemon juice

2¼ cups all-purpose flour

ROYAL ICING

3 tablespoons meringue powder

6 tablespoons warm water, plus more if needed

4 cups confectioners' sugar, sifted

Assorted food colorings (optional)

Assorted colored decorating sugars (optional)

Sprinkles or other decorations (optional)

Vanilla Stars with Chocolate Filling

1¾ cups all-purpose flour

½ teaspoon baking powder

¼ teaspoon salt

½ cup unsalted butter, at room temperature

1 cup sugar

1 large egg

1½ teaspoons vanilla extract

2 oz bittersweet or semisweet chocolate, chopped

2 tablespoons heavy cream

Tempting and classic, these lovely chocolate-layered stars are always popular. For added flavor, brush the solid stars with some beaten egg white and sprinkle with cinnamon sugar before baking.

Preheat oven to 350°F. Lightly grease 3 baking sheets or line them with parchment paper.

In a bowl, combine the flour, baking powder, and salt. Stir until well blended. In a large bowl, using an electric mixer on medium speed, beat the butter and sugar until light and fluffy. Add the egg and vanilla and beat until blended. Reduce the mixer speed to low and gradually beat in the flour mixture just until blended and the dough comes together.

Turn out the dough onto a work surface. Divide in half, then gently gather up each portion and press into a disk. Wrap 1 disk in plastic wrap and set aside. (If the dough is very soft, wrap both disks in plastic wrap and refrigerate until firm, about 30 minutes.)

Sprinkle the work surface with flour. Place the unwrapped disk on the floured surface, and sprinkle the top with a little flour. Roll out the dough ⅛ inch thick, sprinkling more flour under and over the dough as needed to prevent sticking.

Using a 2¾-inch star-shaped cookie cutter, cut out as many stars as possible, cutting them close together. Pull away the scraps of dough from around the shapes and set the scraps aside. Using an offset spatula, carefully transfer the cookies to a prepared baking sheet, spacing them about 1 inch apart. Gather up the reserved dough scraps and gently press them into a disk. Repeat the rolling and cutting process with the scraps and the second dough disk, cutting out 2¾-inch stars as before. Then, using a 1½-inch star-shaped cookie cutter, cut out the centers of these cookies. Transfer the small solid stars to another baking sheet and the cutout cookies to the remaining sheet.

Bake the cookies until lightly browned at the edges, about 8 minutes for the small solid stars, about 9 minutes for the cutout stars, and about 10 minutes for the large solid stars. Let the cookies cool on the baking sheets on a wire rack for 15 minutes, then transfer the cookies to the rack to cool completely.

Combine the chocolate and cream in a small heatproof bowl and heat in microwave or set the bowl over (but not touching) simmering water until the chocolate is melted. Stir until smooth. Spread about ½ teaspoon of the chocolate mixture on the underside of each large solid star cookie and top with a cutout cookie, underside down. Press gently. Set the sandwich cookies on the wire rack until the filling is set, about 20 minutes.

MAKES ABOUT 2 DOZEN SANDWICH COOKIES AND 2 DOZEN SMALL STARS

Toasted Coconut Thumbprint Cookies

1 cup unsalted butter, at room temperature

⅔ cup sugar

¼ teaspoon salt

2 large eggs, separated

1 teaspoon vanilla extract

¼ teaspoon coconut extract

2½ cups all-purpose flour

2½ cups sweetened shredded dried coconut, toasted (see note)

About ¼ cup apricot or raspberry jam

For this recipe, look for sweetened shredded dried coconut. To toast it, spread it on a rimmed baking sheet and bake in a 325°F oven, stirring once or twice, until golden, about 8 minutes.

Preheat oven to 350°F. Have ready 2 ungreased baking sheets or line with parchment paper.

In a large bowl, using an electric mixer on medium speed, beat the butter, sugar, and salt until light and fluffy. Add the egg yolks and the vanilla and coconut extracts and beat until well blended. Reduce the mixer speed to low and gradually beat in the flour just until blended. Place the toasted coconut in a shallow bowl. Lightly beat the egg whites.

Using lightly floured hands, shape the dough into 1-inch balls. Dip each ball in the egg whites and then roll evenly in the coconut, pressing to help it adhere. Arrange the balls about 1 inch apart on the baking sheets. Press a fingertip into the center of each ball to make a small indentation (if the dough is sticky, coat your finger with flour). Spoon about ¼ teaspoon of the jam into each hollow.

Bake the cookies until the tops look dry, 10–12 minutes. Let the cookies cool on the baking sheets for 15 minutes, then transfer to a wire rack to cool completely.

MAKES ABOUT 3 DOZEN COOKIES

Chocolate Shortbread

Shortbread, a specialty of Scotland, tastes best when it is both noticeably rich and delicately crumbly.

Preheat oven to 325°F. Lightly grease a straight-sided 9-inch square baking pan and line the bottom and sides with parchment paper.

In a bowl, sift together the flour and cocoa powder and set aside. In a large bowl, using an electric mixer on medium speed, beat the butter, confectioners' sugar, and salt until light and fluffy. Add the vanilla and beat until blended. Reduce the mixer speed to low and gradually beat in the sifted flour-cocoa mixture just until blended.

Scrape the dough into the prepared baking pan. Using lightly floured fingertips, pat the dough into an even layer. Using a ruler and a knife, score the dough into 1-by-2¼-inch bars. Positioning the tines of a fork on an angle, prick each bar twice all the way through the dough. Bake until the top appears dry, 38–40 minutes.

Transfer the pan to a wire rack until cool enough to handle yet still warm, 5–7 minutes. Using the score marks as a guide, cut the bars through to the pan bottom and let cool in the pan. Using the parchment, lift the pieces from the pan.

MAKES 3 DOZEN BARS

1¾ cups all-purpose flour

⅓ cup unsweetened cocoa powder

1 cup unsalted butter, at room temperature

1¼ cups confectioners' sugar

¼ teaspoon salt

1 teaspoon vanilla extract

Toasted Pecan Butter Cookies

1 cup unsalted butter, at room temperature

⅔ cup sugar

Pinch of salt

1 teaspoon vanilla extract

2¼ cups all-purpose flour

⅔ cup chopped pecans, toasted (see below)

TOASTING NUTS

Toasting intensifies the flavor and aroma of nuts by releasing their natural oils. To toast any kind of nut, preheat oven to 350°F and spread the nuts in a single layer on a rimmed baking sheet. Bake, stirring occasionally, until the nuts are fragrant and have darkened, 5–10 minutes, depending on the type of nut. Let cool before using.

Pecans, which are native to North America and cultivated primarily in the American South, are harvested in the fall, making them a popular ingredient in all kinds of holiday sweets, from cookies and candies to pies and cakes.

In a large bowl, using an electric mixer on medium speed, beat the butter, sugar, and salt until light and fluffy. Add the vanilla and beat until well blended. Reduce the mixer speed to low and gradually beat in the flour and pecans just until blended.

Turn out the dough onto a large sheet of plastic wrap. Use the plastic wrap to shape the dough into a log about 8 inches long and 2 inches in diameter. Wrap the log in a second sheet of plastic wrap and refrigerate until firm, about 3 hours.

Preheat oven to 350°F. Line 3 baking sheets with parchment paper.

Unwrap the chilled dough and, using a thin, sharp knife, cut the log into slices ¼ inch thick. Arrange the slices 1 inch apart on the prepared baking sheets. Bake the cookies until golden brown around the edges, about 14 minutes. Let cool on the baking sheets for 15 minutes, then transfer to a wire rack to cool completely.

MAKES ABOUT 3 DOZEN COOKIES

Mexican Wedding Cookies

1 cup unsalted butter, at room temperature

1½ cups confectioners' sugar

¼ teaspoon salt

Pinch of ground cinnamon

1½ teaspoons vanilla extract

2 cups all-purpose flour

½ cup finely chopped walnuts or pecans, toasted (see above)

Also known as Russian tea cakes or pecan puffs, these melt-in-your-mouth cookies are a perennial holiday favorite. They keep well for up to 1 week when layered between sheets of waxed paper in an airtight container.

Preheat oven to 325°F. Line 2 baking sheets with parchment paper.

In a large bowl, using an electric mixer on medium speed, beat the butter, ¾ cup of the confectioners' sugar, the salt, and the cinnamon until light and fluffy. Add the vanilla and beat until well blended. Reduce the mixer speed to medium-low and gradually beat in the flour and nuts just until blended.

Using lightly floured hands, shape the dough into 1½-inch balls and place 1 inch apart on the prepared baking sheets. Bake until light golden brown on the bottom, about 20 minutes. Let cool briefly on the baking sheets, about 5 minutes. Sift the remaining ¾ cup confectioners' sugar into a shallow bowl. Roll the warm cookies in the confectioners' sugar until evenly coated. Set the cookies on a wire rack to cool completely.

MAKES ABOUT 2½ DOZEN COOKIES

Raspberry and Hazelnut Linzer Bars

1⅔ cups all-purpose flour

1⅓ cups ground hazelnuts, toasted
(see page 40)

1 teaspoon ground cinnamon

½ teaspoon ground cloves

¼ teaspoon salt

1 cup unsalted butter, at room temperature

1½ cups sugar

½ teaspoon grated lemon zest

2 large eggs

1 cup seedless raspberry preserves

These layered cookies call for many of the same ingredients used in the famed Linzertorte, thus their name.

Preheat oven to 350°F. Lightly grease a 9-by-13-inch baking pan. Line the bottom and sides with parchment paper, then lightly grease and flour the paper.

In a bowl, stir together the flour, hazelnuts, cinnamon, cloves, and salt. In a large bowl, using an electric mixer on medium speed, beat the butter, sugar, and lemon zest until light and fluffy. Add the eggs, one at a time, and beat just until blended. Reduce the mixer speed to low and add the flour mixture in 2 batches, beating well after each addition.

Scoop two-thirds of the dough into the prepared baking pan. Using lightly floured fingertips, pat the dough into an even layer. Spread the preserves evenly over the dough. Dollop the remaining dough in spoonfuls over the preserves. Press the dough with floured fingers to flatten slightly. The top dough layer should not cover the preserves completely. Bake until the top is browned and the preserves are bubbling, about 50 minutes. Transfer to a wire rack and let cool completely. Using the parchment, lift out the whole cookie and transfer to a cutting board. Trim away the edges (about ½ inch on all sides) and cut into 2-inch squares. If desired, cut each square into 2 triangles.

MAKES 2 DOZEN SQUARES OR 4 DOZEN TRIANGLES

Ginger Crisps

As they bake, these spice-laden cookies fill your kitchen with an irresistible aroma. Store them in an airtight container so they remain crisp.

In a bowl, combine the flour, ginger, cinnamon, nutmeg, baking soda, and salt. Stir until well blended. In a large bowl, using an electric mixer on medium speed, beat the butter and sugar until light and fluffy. Add the egg yolk and molasses and beat until well blended. Reduce the mixer speed to medium-low and gradually beat in the flour mixture until the dough is well blended and forms moist pebbles.

Turn out the dough onto a lightly floured work surface. Knead gently until smooth. Shape into a squared-off log 8 inches long. Wrap in plastic wrap and refrigerate until firm, about 3 hours.

Preheat oven to 350°F. Line 2 baking sheets with parchment paper.

Unwrap the chilled dough and, using a thin, sharp knife, cut the log into slices ¼ inch thick. Arrange the slices about 1 inch apart on the prepared baking sheets. Bake the cookies until slightly darker brown around the edges, about 10 minutes. Let cool for 15 minutes on the baking sheets, then transfer to a wire rack to cool completely.

MAKES ABOUT 3 DOZEN COOKIES

1⅔ cups all-purpose flour

1 teaspoon ground ginger

¾ teaspoon ground cinnamon

Pinch of freshly grated nutmeg

½ teaspoon baking soda

¼ teaspoon salt

½ cup unsalted butter, at room temperature

⅔ cup firmly packed golden brown sugar

1 large egg yolk

2 tablespoons unsulfured light molasses

GIFTS FROM THE HOLIDAY KITCHEN

Homemade treats, created in your kitchen and wrapped up in pretty packages, are a wonderful way to share the joy of Christmas. Do not worry if you failed to spend time during the year putting up preserves in preparation for holiday gift giving. There are many easy, edible treasures you can make as the season approaches. Devote an afternoon to cooking up a big batch of sweet and savory goodies, or, if you are pressed for time, buy Christmas candies to fill colorful holiday gift cones.

The secret to transforming homemade foods into festive gifts is the presentation. Look for interesting boxes, jars, baskets, and galvanized tins at garden and hardware stores, packaging stores, and restaurant wholesalers. They do not need to be expensive or fancy, because you will be dressing them up. Ribbon, brightly colored tissue or cellophane, and hand-lettered gift tags are all you need to create a whimsical gift that is sure to be greeted with a smile. For a special touch, incorporate an extra little "keeper" gift into the packaging that relates to the food inside, such as an attractive serving spoon or a miniature tart tin.

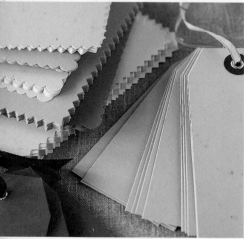

RECIPES

Tangerine Curd

Cheese Straws

Parmesan Palmiers

Hazelnut Brittle

Cranberry Chutney

Cherries in Brandy

Prunes in Brandy

PLANNING AHEAD

1 WEEK AHEAD

Organize gift list

Gather jars and other gift containers

Collect colorful ribbons and cards

Buy cellophane, tissue, and other gift papers

1 DAY AHEAD

Thaw puff pastry

Write holiday labels

Make brittle

1 HOUR AHEAD

Toast nuts

Sterilize jars and lids

Holiday Candy Cones

CONES ‹ CANDIES • CELLOPHANE • RIBBON

When you are pressed for time, these festive candy cones, which rely on store-bought sweets and easy-to-find decorative wrappings, are ideal holiday gifts.

ONE Gather together all your supplies: one or more types of holiday candy, decorative cones, a roll of cellophane, and seasonal ribbon.

TWO Cut squares of cellophane about twice the size of the cone. Carefully wrap each cone, using tape or glue to adhere the edges of the cellophane to the cone. Leave plenty of cellophane at the top to cover the sweets.

THREE Fill each cone with sweets, mixing varieties if desired. Gather the cellophane just above the sweets, twist gently, and then tie with a colorful bow. Attractively trim the top of the cellophane.

Tangerine Curd

Most citrus fruits are harvested in the winter months, which makes this rich, smooth curd made from tangerines an ideal Christmastime gift. The term tangerine *is typically used for any mandarin orange with deep-colored skin. If tangerines are unavailable, you can substitute tangelos, which are a cross between a mandarin and a grapefruit or pomelo.*

In a small saucepan, bring the tangerine zest and juice and lemon juice to a boil over high heat. Cook, stirring occasionally, until reduced to ¾ cup, about 20 minutes. Let cool.

In a stainless-steel or other nonreactive heatproof bowl set over (but not touching) simmering water, whisk together the whole eggs, egg yolks, and sugar until the mixture is thick and a pale lemon color, 6–7 minutes.

Add the butter, 1 cube at a time, stirring until it has completely melted before adding the next cube. Add the reduced juice and zest mixture and whisk to combine. Cook, whisking, just until the mixture has thickened enough to coat the back of a spoon, about 3 minutes. Do not let the mixture boil.

Ladle the hot curd into sterilized jars (see right), wipe the rims clean, and seal tightly with lids. Let cool completely, about 30 minutes, then refrigerate. The curd can be stored, refrigerated, for up to 2 weeks.

MAKES 3 HALF-PINTS

Grated zest of 6 tangerines

3 cups fresh tangerine juice

½ cup fresh lemon juice

3 large whole eggs, plus 2 large egg yolks, at room temperature

½ cup sugar

⅔ cup unsalted butter, at room temperature, cut into ½-inch cubes

HOW TO STERILIZE JARS AND LIDS

Sterilizing jars and lids is easy and helps safeguard against spoilage. Thoroughly wash the jars and their lids in hot, soapy water and rinse well. Place the jars upright in a large pot. Fill the pot with hot water, covering the jars by 1 inch. Cover the pot, bring to a boil, and boil vigorously for 10 minutes at altitudes of 1,000 feet or less; add an additional minute of boiling time for each 1,000 feet of elevation gain. Remove the pot from the heat and leave the jars in hot water until ready to use. Place washed and rinsed lids in a small saucepan. Add water to cover, bring to a boil, and remove from the heat. Leave the lids in hot water until ready to use.

Cheese Straws

Zesty, savory cheese straws make an easy and elegant holiday gift. To save time, store-bought puff pastry is used for the dough.

Preheat oven to 400°F. Line 2 baking sheets with parchment paper. In a bowl, toss together the cheeses, dry mustard, cayenne, and black pepper.

Working with 1 pastry sheet at a time, on a lightly floured surface, gently roll out the sheet into a 12-by-10-inch rectangle. Brush with the egg and sprinkle with ½ cup of the cheese mixture. Flip the sheet so the cheese side is underneath, then brush the top with egg and sprinkle with another ½ cup of the cheese mixture.

Using a fluted pastry or pizza wheel, cut the sheet into 24 strips each ½ inch wide and about 10 inches long. One at a time, twist the strips and set at least 1 inch apart on a prepared baking sheet, pressing the ends onto the parchment to secure them and prevent untwisting. Repeat with the remaining ingredients and second pastry sheet.

Bake until the cheese melts and the straws turn crisp and golden, about 15 minutes. Transfer to a wire rack to cool. Store in an airtight container for up to 2 weeks.

MAKES ABOUT 4 DOZEN STRAWS

CHEESE STRAWS

1 cup finely shredded cheddar cheese

1 cup grated Parmesan or pecorino cheese

1 tablespoon dry mustard

½ teaspoon cayenne pepper

½ teaspoon freshly ground black pepper

1 package (17 oz) frozen puff pastry (2 sheets), thawed in the refrigerator and unfolded

1 egg, lightly beaten

PARMESAN PALMIERS

1 cup grated Parmesan cheese

1 cup grated pecorino cheese

2 teaspoons dry mustard

½–1 teaspoon cayenne pepper, to taste

¼ teaspoon freshly ground black pepper

1 package (17 oz) frozen puff pastry (2 sheets), thawed in the refrigerator and unfolded

Parmesan Palmiers

Palmiers are French palm leaf–shaped cookies made from sweetened puff pastry. Here, the distinctive shape has been borrowed for making peppery cheese appetizers.

In a bowl, toss together the cheeses, dry mustard, cayenne, and black pepper.

Working with 1 pastry sheet at a time, on a lightly floured surface, gently roll out the sheet into a 10-by-9¼-inch rectangle. Sprinkle with about ¾ cup of the cheese mixture. Starting from a long side, lightly roll up the pastry, stopping at the midpoint of the sheet. Roll up the other long side the same way, to meet in the center. Repeat with the remaining pastry sheet and ¾ cup of the cheese mixture. Wrap each roll tightly in plastic wrap, place on a baking sheet, and refrigerate or freeze until firm.

Preheat oven to 400°F. Line 2 baking sheets with parchment paper. Working with 1 pastry roll at a time, and using a thin, sharp knife, cut off and discard a thin slice from each end to form an even edge. Cut into slices about ½ inch thick. If the dough begins to feel too soft and unmanageable, just rewrap it and refrigerate for 30 minutes. Arrange the *palmiers* flat, 2 inches apart, on the prepared baking sheets. Sprinkle with the remaining cheese mixture, along with any cheese that has fallen out. Bake until the cheese melts and the pastry is crisp and golden outside and fully cooked inside, 12–15 minutes. Transfer to a wire rack to cool. Serve slightly warm or at room temperature. Store in an airtight container for up to 2 weeks.

MAKES ABOUT 3 DOZEN SMALL PALMIERS

Hazelnut Brittle

You need only a few commonplace tools to make this candy: a heavy-bottomed saucepan, a candy thermometer, and a heavy-duty rimmed baking sheet. Dry weather with low humidity helps, too. Use packaged chopped hazelnuts to avoid the added step of toasting and removing their skins.

Preheat oven to 350°F. Lightly spray a 12-by-17-inch rimmed baking sheet with vegetable oil cooking spray.

Spread the hazelnuts on an ungreased baking sheet or in a shallow pan. Bake, stirring once or twice, until the nuts are fragrant but have not darkened, 4–5 minutes.

Meanwhile, in a large, heavy saucepan with a candy thermometer clipped to the side, combine the sugar, corn syrup, and ½ cup water over medium heat, stirring until the sugar is dissolved and bubbles just begin to rise and break on the surface. Continue to cook, without stirring, until the temperature reaches 280°F (soft crack).

Add the hot nuts and cook, stirring, until the temperature reaches 305°F (hard crack) and the caramel has turned a golden amber. Remove from the heat and stir in the butter, baking soda, and vanilla. Stir until the butter is completely melted and incorporated. Immediately pour the mixture onto the oiled baking sheet and, using an offset spatula, spread it evenly to the edges of the pan.

Let the brittle cool for 5 minutes. Place a sheet of parchment paper on a work surface. Then flip the pan, slam it down to release brittle, and break brittle into rough 1-inch pieces using your hands or the dull side of a knife blade. Let cool completely. Store in an airtight container in a cool, dry place for up to 2 weeks.

MAKES ABOUT 100 SMALL PIECES

4 cups chopped, skinned hazelnuts

2 cups sugar

¾ cup light corn syrup

½ cup water

¾ cup unsalted butter, cut into ½-inch cubes

2 teaspoons baking soda

1 teaspoon vanilla extract

Cranberry Chutney

½ cup cider vinegar

½ cup water

2 cups firmly packed dark brown sugar

3½ cups fresh cranberries

1 cup dried cranberries

1 cup golden raisins

¼ cup crystallized ginger, chopped

2 tablespoons grated orange zest

1 cup fresh orange juice

2 large Granny Smith apples, peeled, cored, and cut into ¼-inch cubes

1 tablespoon vanilla extract

2 teaspoons ground cinnamon

½ teaspoon ground cloves

½ teaspoon ground allspice

1 cup chopped walnuts, toasted (see page 40)

Pack this aromatic chutney into half-pint jars, then cover the lids with fabric or tie a ribbon around the neck. If possible, include the recipe and tips on serving—with ham, duck, or even pâté—with each jar.

In a large saucepan, bring the vinegar, water, and brown sugar to a boil over medium heat, stirring until the sugar is dissolved. Stir in the fresh cranberries, dried cranberries, raisins, crystallized ginger, orange zest, orange juice, apples, vanilla, cinnamon, cloves, and allspice. Bring to a boil and cook, stirring, until the fresh cranberries pop and the mixture thickens, 15–20 minutes.

Remove from the heat and stir in the walnuts. Ladle the hot chutney into sterilized jars (see page 51), filling almost to the top. Wipe the rims clean and seal tightly with lids. Let cool completely, about 30 minutes, then refrigerate. The chutney can be stored, refrigerated, for up to 2 months.

MAKES ABOUT 6 HALF-PINTS

Cherries in Brandy

*The season for cherries is short, but if you plan ahead, they can be savored
well into winter by preserving them in brandy. Traditionally, tart cherries such
as Morello or Montmorency are used. Spoon the cherries, with or without their
cherry-flavored brandy, over vanilla ice cream or pound cake.*

1 lb cherries (see note), with stems intact

½ cup sugar

About 1 cup brandy

Trim the cherry stems to 1 inch. Using a toothpick or heavy darning needle, prick each
cherry 6 or 7 times. Pack the cherries tightly into a sterilized widemouthed 1-pint jar with
lid (see page 51). Sprinkle the sugar over the cherries. Pour in enough brandy to cover the
fruit completely. Wipe the rim clean and seal tightly with the lid. Store in a cool, dark
place for at least 3 months before using; the cherries will keep for up to 1 year.

MAKES 1 PINT

Prunes in Brandy

*Choose large, meaty prunes, pitted if desired, for this recipe. The brandy
is absorbed and combines with the natural sweetness of the fruit to make
plump morsels that explode with flavor. Enjoy the prunes by themselves
with an espresso, or spoon them and their juices over vanilla ice cream.
For recipe photo, see page 47.*

⅓ lb large prunes

⅓ cup sugar

½ cinnamon stick

2 long strips orange zest

2 long strips lemon zest

About 1 cup brandy

Pack the prunes tightly into a sterilized widemouthed 1-pint jar with lid (see page 51).
Sprinkle the sugar over the prunes. Tuck the cinnamon stick and strips of citrus zest down
into the jar, keeping them next to the glass so the color is visible. Pour in enough brandy
to cover the fruit completely. Wipe the rim clean and seal tightly with the lid. Store in a
cool, dark place for at least 3 months before using; the prunes will keep for up to 1 year.

MAKES 1 PINT

COZY FIRESIDE CHRISTMAS EVE SUPPER

The lighting of the Yule log is a longtime Christmas Eve tradition, and an enduring symbol of the warmth associated with the holiday. Celebrate that tradition with an intimate fireside supper that brings together your family and closest friends for a moment of tranquility amid the bustle of the holidays.

Start by moving the dining table in front of the hearth and dressing it with your best white tablecloth. White, silver, and forest green make an inviting, wintry color palette for the table and the room. Put together a charming—and easy—seasonal centerpiece by filling glass vases and containers with ornaments, flowers, fruits, and nuts. Augment the arrangement with votive or other short candles.

Decorate the mantel with boughs of greenery, miniature potted evergreens, and candles of different heights to add visual interest. Dim overhead lighting, so that candlelight and firelight provide most of the illumination. At each setting, place a whimsical gift, wrapped in silver paper, with a name tag that doubles as a place card. Start the meal with a sparkling toast: a Prosecco aperitif that goes perfectly with the shrimp.

MENU

*Roasted Shrimp with
Black Pepper and Thyme*

Sautéed Mushroom Salad

*Salt and Fennel
Roasted Pork Loin*

Roasted Fingerlings and Shallots

*Green Beans with
Pine Nuts and Crisp Pancetta*

*Dried-Apricot Clafouti
with Mascarpone
and Sugared Almonds*

*Pistachio and Dried-Cherry
Biscotti Dipped in
Dark Chocolate*

PLANNING AHEAD

1 WEEK AHEAD

Bake biscotti

Wrap gifts for place settings

1 DAY AHEAD

Ready centerpieces except roses

Prepare pork with salt rub

Cook green beans

3 HOURS AHEAD

Trim roses

Combine ingredients for shrimp

Clean mushrooms

Cook apricots and almonds

JUST BEFORE SERVING

Roast pork

Roast potatoes

Assemble salad

A Shimmering Table

GLASS VASES • SEASONAL OBJECTS • FLOWERS • CANDLES

An array of glass containers showcases colorful seasonal objects in this simple, elegant centerpiece for your holiday table.

ONE Gather clear glass containers of different heights and a cornucopia of colorful and textured items, like crab apples, silvered almonds, almonds in the shell, pine cones, Christmas ornaments, white roses, and candles.

TWO Fill each glass container with a different item, matching sizes. For instance, use shorter vases for small crab apples and votive candles and taller ones for nuts, flowers, and pillar candles.

THREE Arrange the glass vases along the center of your table, staggering the heights and intermixing the candles with the other objects.

Roasted Shrimp with Black Pepper and Thyme

2 lb large shrimp in the shell

¼ cup extra-virgin olive oil

1 tablespoon coarsely chopped fresh thyme, plus sprigs for garnish

2 cloves garlic, minced

Coarse salt and freshly ground pepper

These "shell as you eat" shrimp could not be simpler to make. You can combine all the ingredients up to 3 hours ahead, and cover and refrigerate until it is time to cook. Make sure to accompany the shrimp with plenty of napkins.

Preheat oven to 450°F. Using small kitchen scissors, and starting at the head end, split each shrimp along the back, cutting through the shell, yet keeping the shrimp in one piece. Remove and discard the black vein and put the shrimp in a large bowl.

Drizzle the shrimp with the olive oil and sprinkle with the chopped thyme, garlic, 1 tablespoon salt, and 1 teaspoon pepper. Stir to coat the shrimp, then spread them on a large rimmed baking sheet.

Roast until the shells turn pink and the flesh is opaque, 5–7 minutes. Serve hot or warm and garnish with a thyme sprig.

MAKES 6–8 SERVINGS

Sautéed Mushroom Salad

This robust mushroom salad combines the bold flavors of blue cheese and arugula with a hint of anchovy. Chanterelle, porcino, and oyster are a good combination, or you can mix portobello and cremini with whatever wild mushrooms you can find. Make sure the mushrooms are free of grit. If they are very dirty, rinse them briefly in cold water and quickly pat dry.

In a small jar with a lid, combine the vinegar, shallot, cream, mustard, ¾ teaspoon salt, and ¼ teaspoon pepper. Add the walnut oil, cover, shake well, and set aside.

In a large frying pan over medium-high heat, warm the olive oil. Add the garlic and anchovies and cook, stirring, for 30 seconds. Add the mushrooms, 1 teaspoon salt, and ½ teaspoon pepper and sauté until the mushrooms are tender and most of their liquid has evaporated, 8–10 minutes. Stir in the parsley and remove from the heat.

In a large bowl, toss the arugula with the dressing. Divide among individual plates and top with the warm mushroom mixture. Scatter the cheese over the top and serve at once.

MAKES 6–8 SERVINGS

2 tablespoons sherry vinegar

1 large shallot, minced

1 tablespoon heavy cream

¼ teaspoon Dijon mustard

Coarse salt and freshly ground pepper

¼ cup walnut oil

¼ cup extra-virgin olive oil

2 cloves garlic, minced

4 anchovy fillets, minced

1½ lb assorted fresh mushrooms, brushed clean and thinly sliced (see note)

3 tablespoons chopped fresh flat-leaf parsley

2 bunches arugula, tough stems removed

2 oz Gorgonzola or Roquefort cheese, crumbled

Salt and Fennel Roasted Pork Loin

Your kitchen will fill with the fragrance of fennel while this pork loin roasts. Buy a dry Orvieto or Verdicchio to make the simple pan sauce, and enjoy the rest of the wine with the meal. Ask the butcher for the rack of rib bones from the loin. Cut the ribs apart and add them to the bottom of the pan, where they will bathe in the wine, becoming a wonderful treat for the cook and any helpers.

On a cutting board, chop the garlic and 1 teaspoon salt together to form a paste. Transfer to a small bowl and stir in 1 tablespoon plus 2 teaspoons salt, the rosemary, fennel seeds, and 1½ teaspoons pepper. Rub the pork all over with the salt mixture. Transfer to a platter, cover, and refrigerate for at least 12 hours or up to 24 hours. Remove from the refrigerator 3 hours before cooking, to bring to room temperature.

Preheat oven to 450°F. Drizzle the pork with the olive oil. Place on a V-shaped rack in a roasting pan and scatter the rack bones on the bottom of the pan. Pour in ½ cup of the wine. Roast for 15 minutes, then reduce oven temperature to 350°F. Add another ½ cup wine and roast for 30 minutes longer. Pour in another ½ cup wine and roast until an instant-read thermometer inserted into the meat reads 145°–150°F, 30–40 minutes longer. Transfer the pork and bones to a cutting board and cover loosely with aluminum foil. Let rest for 15 minutes.

Remove the V-shaped rack and place the roasting pan over high heat. Add the remaining ½ cup wine and bring to a boil, scraping up any browned bits from the pan bottom. Add the broth, return to a boil, and cook until the sauce is reduced by half, 3–4 minutes. Strain into a sauce boat.

Garnish the platter with herb sprigs and carve the pork into thin slices before plating. Serve the pan sauce on the side.

MAKES 6–8 SERVINGS

2 cloves garlic, finely minced

Coarse salt

2 tablespoons finely chopped fresh rosemary

2 tablespoons fennel seeds, coarsely crushed

Freshly ground pepper

1 center-cut boneless pork loin, 4 lb, with a thin layer of fat intact and the rack bones separated (see note)

1 tablespoon extra-virgin olive oil

2 cups dry white wine

1 cup chicken broth

Fresh herb sprigs, for garnish

Roasted Fingerlings and Shallots

Fingerlings are slender, wonderfully knobby small potatoes that are just perfect for this dish. There are many varieties, but most are firm and richly flavored when roasted, nicely offsetting the tender, sweet shallots. If fingerlings are unavailable, use the smallest Yellow Finn, red, or similar potatoes you can find, and cut them in half crosswise.

2 lb small fingerling potatoes, cut in half lengthwise

Coarse salt

1 lb shallots, peeled and cut in half through root end

3 tablespoons extra-virgin olive oil

1 tablespoon chopped fresh oregano

Freshly ground pepper

Preheat oven to 450°F. Place the potatoes in a large saucepan with cold water to cover by 1 inch and add 2 teaspoons salt. Bring to a boil over high heat, then reduce to a simmer and cook until the potatoes are still firm but easily pierced with the tip of a knife, 5–7 minutes. Drain well.

In a bowl, combine the shallots, 1 tablespoon of the olive oil, half of the oregano, and ½ teaspoon each salt and pepper. Toss to coat the shallots evenly. Spread on a large, rimmed baking sheet and roast for 5 minutes.

Meanwhile, in a bowl, toss the drained potatoes with the remaining olive oil, remaining oregano, 1 teaspoon salt, and ½ teaspoon pepper. Add to the pan with the shallots and roast until crisp and browned, 15–20 minutes. Serve hot.

MAKES 6–8 SERVINGS

Green Beans with Pine Nuts and Crisp Pancetta

When shopping for beans, look for intensely green pods and taut skins. Trim off only the stem, where the bean was attached to the plant, and leave the elegantly pointed tip intact. You can cook the beans a day ahead, plunge them into ice water, drain, and refrigerate in a zippered plastic bag. Just before serving, finish them in the pan with the pine nuts and pancetta.

1½ lb green beans, trimmed

Coarse salt

2 tablespoons olive oil

¼ lb thinly sliced pancetta, diced

¼ cup pine nuts

1 teaspoon grated lemon zest

Freshly ground pepper

Bring a large saucepan three-fourths full of water to a boil. Add the beans and 2 teaspoons salt and cook until tender-crisp, 6–8 minutes. Drain well.

In a large frying pan over medium-high heat, warm the olive oil. Add the pancetta and cook, stirring occasionally, until crisp, 6–8 minutes. Using a slotted spoon, transfer to a small plate. Add the pine nuts to the pan and sauté until lightly browned, 1–2 minutes. Return the pancetta to the pan and add the beans, lemon zest, and ½ teaspoon each salt and pepper. Toss to combine and cook only until the beans are heated through. Serve hot.

MAKES 6–8 SERVINGS

Dried-Apricot Clafouti with Mascarpone and Sugared Almonds

Traditionally, this simple French dessert, typically described as a cross between a pancake and a custard, is filled with cherries. Here, the cherries are replaced by plump, Gewürztraminer-soused dried apricots. Each serving is garnished with dollops of honeyed mascarpone and a crown of sugared almonds. If mascarpone is unavailable, substitute equal parts sour cream and cream cheese.

Preheat oven to 350°F. Grease a 9-inch shallow round baking dish or pie dish.

In a saucepan, combine the apricots, wine or apple juice, and ⅓ cup of the sugar. Bring to a boil over medium-high heat, stirring to dissolve the sugar, and cook until the wine is reduced to ¼ cup, 7–9 minutes.

Meanwhile, in a bowl, whisk 1 egg into the flour until smooth, then whisk in the remaining eggs, milk, almond extract, and salt. Using a slotted spoon, transfer the apricots to the prepared baking dish, spreading them out evenly. Pour the ¼ cup reduced wine into the batter, add the remaining ⅓ cup sugar, stir well, and slowly pour the batter over the apricots, being careful not to dislodge them.

Bake the clafouti until it is puffed and golden brown, about 35 minutes. Let cool on a wire rack for 10 minutes.

While the clafouti is cooling, in a small bowl, stir the honey into the mascarpone and set aside.

To make the sugared almonds, in a large frying pan over medium-high heat, melt the butter. Add 1 tablespoon of the sugar and the almonds and cook, stirring, until the almonds are evenly coated and lightly browned, 1–2 minutes. Transfer to a bowl and toss with the remaining 1 tablespoon sugar.

To serve, cut the warm clafouti into wedges and place in individual goblets or on plates. Top each serving with a dollop of mascarpone and a sprinkle of almonds.

MAKES 6–8 SERVINGS

2 cups dried apricots

1 cup Gewürztraminer wine or apple juice

⅔ cup sugar

3 large eggs

⅓ cup all-purpose flour

½ cup whole milk

2 teaspoons almond extract

⅛ teaspoon salt

2½ tablespoons honey

1 cup mascarpone cheese

SUGARED ALMONDS

2 tablespoons unsalted butter

2 tablespoons sugar

½ cup sliced almonds

Pistachio and Dried-Cherry Biscotti Dipped in Dark Chocolate

2 cups all-purpose flour

1 teaspoon baking powder

¼ teaspoon salt

1 cup sugar

2 teaspoons grated orange zest

½ cup unsalted butter, at room temperature

2 large eggs

1 teaspoon vanilla extract

¾ cup unsalted pistachio nuts, toasted (see page 40) and coarsely chopped

½ cup dried tart cherries, coarsely chopped

6 oz bittersweet or semisweet chocolate, 4 oz coarsely chopped, 2 oz in large chunks

1 tablespoon walnut oil

Accompany these merry green-and-red-flecked biscotti with a glass of vin santo or a cup of espresso. They will keep well in an airtight container for a week. Without the chocolate, you can freeze the biscotti for up to a month; bring them to room temperature before dipping them in chocolate.

Preheat oven to 350°F. Line a baking sheet with parchment paper. Have ready another unlined baking sheet.

In a bowl, stir together the flour, baking powder, and salt. In a food processor, combine the sugar and orange zest and process until finely chopped. Transfer the sugar mixture to a large bowl, add the butter, and, using an electric mixer on medium speed, beat until light and fluffy. Add the eggs, one at a time, beating well after each addition. Beat in the vanilla. Reduce the mixer speed to low and gradually beat in the flour mixture just until blended. Using a rubber spatula, fold in the pistachios and dried cherries.

Divide the dough in half and place both portions on the parchment-lined baking sheet. Quickly form each half into a log 12 inches long and 2 inches in diameter. Place the logs at least 3 inches apart on the baking sheet and smooth them with dampened fingers. Bake the logs, rotating the pan 180 degrees halfway through the baking time, until the logs begin to crack on top, about 35 minutes. Remove from oven and let cool on the baking sheet for 10 minutes. Leave the oven set at 350°F.

Transfer the logs to a cutting board and discard the parchment. Using a sharp, serrated knife, cut each log on the diagonal into slices ½ inch wide. Arrange the slices flat on the 2 unlined baking sheets. Bake until lightly browned on both sides, about 16 minutes. Let the cookies cool on the baking sheets on a wire rack. Arrange the cooled slices in neat rows on the sheets, each cookie barely touching the next.

While the biscotti are cooling, melt the 4 oz chopped chocolate with the walnut oil in the top of a double boiler set over (but not touching) simmering water. (Alternatively, heat them in a glass bowl in the microwave for 1 minute, stirring after 30 seconds.) Off the heat, add the remaining large chunks of chocolate and stir just until the mixture is barely warm. Remove any unmelted large chunks. At an angle, quickly dip one end of each cookie into the chocolate mixture, then return it to the baking sheet. Let stand until the chocolate is completely set, about 30 minutes.

MAKES 4 DOZEN BISCOTTI

GREAT LAKES CHRISTMAS BREAKFAST

Christmas morning often means a big family gathering. Instead of an impromptu meal, serve a hearty Scandinavian-style holiday breakfast buffet inspired by the Yuletide traditions of the Nordic settlers who arrived in the Great Lakes Region in the late 1880s. The entire menu, except for the eggs, can be prepared ahead of time. The night before, set the table, then arrange all the platters and serving utensils you will need on the sideboard or kitchen island that will serve as the buffet. Once you have mapped out the buffet, you can bring the platters to the kitchen, where they will be ready to be filled in the morning.

Keep the decor bright and simple, evoking the sparkle of a snowy Scandinavian morning. A natural wood table with an ice-blue runner is an inviting backdrop for tall, white winter blooms, sprays of pine and red berries in miniature galvanized tubs, and modern dishes. Affix a sprig of pine and berries tied with ribbon to each chair, and put a homemade, treat-filled Christmas cracker or small wrapped gift at each place setting. At serving time, arrange the food on the platters, scramble the eggs, and serve freshly squeezed orange juice, along with coffee, tea, and cocoa.

MENU

Scrambled Eggs and Chives

*Bacon Glazed with Brown Sugar
and Cardamom*

*Gravlax with Sweet Mustard
and Dill Sauce*

Swedish Limpa Bread

*Beet and Apple Salad
with Grapefruit*

Watercress and Radish Salad

Kugelhopf

Gingerbread with Lemon Cream

PLANNING AHEAD

2 DAYS AHEAD

Make Christmas crackers

Collect sprigs of pine and red berries

Prepare gravlax and rotate 2 or 3 times

Make dill sauce

1 DAY AHEAD

Rotate gravlax 2 or 3 times

Bake limpa bread

Roast beets

Peel and cut apples

Bake gingerbread

Bake kugelhopf

1 HOUR AHEAD

Slice gravlax

Make salads

Whip cream for gingerbread

Slice limpa bread

Christmas Crackers

CARDBOARD ROLLS • RIBBON • PRIZES • CREPE PAPER • TAPE

You can put one of these festive Christmas crackers, each one concealing a "prize," at each place setting, or pile them all in a basket on the buffet or breakfast table.

ONE Gather all the supplies you will need: Collect paper-towel or toilet-paper rolls and cut as needed into 4–6-inch lengths, or make rolls from sheets of midweight card stock. Buy colorful paper that will hold its shape, such as crepe paper, and decorative ribbon or raffia. Choose small, whimsical objects for the prizes, such as wrapped chocolates or tiny ornaments.

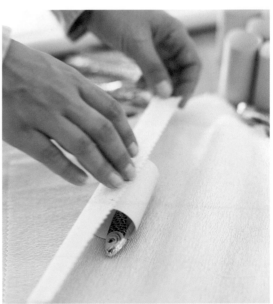

TWO Cut a 10-inch square of crepe paper for each cracker using pinking sheers or scissors. Center the cardboard roll on one edge of the paper, and use a dot of glue or a piece of tape to affix the paper to the roll. Place the prize inside the cylinder. Carefully roll the paper around the cardboard, making a few rotations, and affix the seam with glue or tape.

THREE Tie a ribbon on each end of the cracker. Gently unfurl each end, flaring out the paper into flower bursts.

Scrambled Eggs and Chives

Scrambled eggs are an uncomplicated and trouble-free dish, making them ideal for Christmas morning. Wait until everything else is ready before you begin cooking the eggs, so they will be piping hot when served. Remove them from the heat when slightly underdone, as they will continue to cook.

18 large eggs

¾ cup heavy cream

6 tablespoons snipped fresh chives, plus more for garnish

Coarse salt and freshly ground pepper

6 tablespoons unsalted butter

In each of 2 bowls, briskly whisk together 9 of the eggs, 6 tablespoons of the cream, 3 tablespoons of the chives, ¾ teaspoon salt, and ¾ teaspoon pepper until well blended and the broken yolks streak the whites.

In a large, heavy nonstick frying pan, melt 3 tablespoons of the butter over medium heat. Pour in 1 bowlful of the egg mixture and let cook undisturbed for 2–3 minutes to warm through. Continue to cook, turning over areas of the eggs as they set with a heatproof spatula or wooden spoon, then folding and stirring them into big, soft, fluffy curds until just set and creamy, 5–6 minutes total. Transfer to a warmed platter and keep warm. Repeat with the remaining butter and egg mixture. Garnish with chives and serve hot.

MAKES 10–12 SERVINGS

Bacon Glazed with Brown Sugar and Cardamom

Sizes vary from brand to brand, but count on about 12 strips per pound when buying thick-sliced bacon. Most packaged bacon is not properly cured or smoked, relying instead on smoke flavoring. Ask the butcher for the best-quality bacon; it costs more, but its flavor and texture are worth it.

2 lb thick-sliced bacon

¾ cup firmly packed golden brown sugar

½ teaspoon ground cardamom

Freshly ground pepper

Position a rack in the upper third of oven and another rack in the lower third. Preheat oven to 350°F. Line the bottom and sides of 2 large, rimmed baking sheets with aluminum foil.

Separate the bacon strips and arrange them, without overlapping, on the prepared pans. In a bowl, toss together the brown sugar, cardamom, and ½ teaspoon pepper. Sprinkle the bacon strips evenly with the sugar mixture.

Place 1 pan on the upper oven rack and the other pan on the lower rack. Bake, without turning the bacon, for 25 minutes. Switch the pans between the racks and rotate them 180 degrees. Continue to bake, without turning the bacon, until the strips are dark brown but not quite crisp, 10–15 minutes longer. Using tongs, lift the bacon strips from the pans, gently shaking off the excess drippings, drain briefly on paper towels, and then arrange on a warmed platter. Serve hot.

MAKES 10–12 SERVINGS

Gravlax with Sweet Mustard and Dill Sauce

Gravlax is a well-known Scandinavian salmon preparation in which the fish is cured with a mixture of salt, sugar, dill, and other seasonings. Here, the fish is also rubbed with vodka or aquavit, the latter a popular Scandinavian spirit flavored with caraway seeds. For a close-up view of the dill sauce, see page 87.

GRAVLAX

2 same-sized salmon fillets, 1½ lb each, with skin intact

6 whole lemons, plus 10–12 slices for garnish

½ cup granulated sugar

½ cup coarse salt

3 tablespoons cracked peppercorns

3 tablespoons coriander seeds, lightly crushed

3 tablespoons vodka or aquavit

SAUCE

⅓ cup Dijon mustard

3 tablespoons firmly packed light brown sugar

2 tablespoons cider vinegar

⅓ cup sunflower oil

3 tablespoons finely chopped fresh dill

To make the gravlax, trim any fat from the salmon. Run your fingers gently over the fish to check for small bones, and remove any with sturdy tweezers or needle-nosed pliers.

Finely grate the zest from the 6 lemons, then slice the lemons thinly and discard any seeds. In a bowl, stir together the lemon zest, granulated sugar, salt, peppercorns, and coriander seeds. Rub the vodka or aquavit over the flesh side of the salmon fillets. Coat the flesh sides of both fillets with the peppercorn mixture. Lay 1 fillet, flesh side up, in a glass or ceramic dish just large enough to hold it. Cover the fillet with a layer of lemon slices, then lay the remaining fillet on top, flesh side down. Cover the dish with plastic wrap and top with a piece of cardboard cut slightly smaller than the dish. Weight the salmon evenly with heavy cans of food. Refrigerate for 48 hours, turning 4–6 times and draining away any accumulated liquid. (The heavy weight and the salt will force the liquid out of the fish, leaving it firm and easy to slice.)

To make the sauce, in a small bowl, whisk together the mustard, brown sugar, and vinegar until smooth. Add the oil in a slow, steady stream, whisking constantly until the sauce is emulsified. Stir in the dill. (The sauce may be prepared up to 3 days ahead and refrigerated, tightly covered, until serving.) Before serving, whisk the sauce well and transfer to a small serving bowl.

To serve, unwrap the salmon and scrape off the lemon slices and most of the peppercorn mixture. Using a thin, sharp knife held almost horizontally, cut the salmon on the diagonal into very thin slices. Lift the slices from the skin and arrange on a serving platter. (The salmon may be sliced up to 6 hours ahead and refrigerated, tightly covered, until serving.) Garnish with lemon slices. Serve alongside the sauce.

MAKES 10–12 SERVINGS

Swedish Limpa Bread

This classic Swedish bread is wonderful for Christmas morning. It also makes great sandwiches, especially turkey or ham with cranberry sauce, and is good spread with cream cheese. If you have a Microplane grater, you will need 3 large oranges for the zest; without it, you will need 4 oranges. To ensure the best flavor, freshly grind all the spices.

In a large saucepan, bring the beer just to a boil over medium-high heat. Remove from the heat and add the butter or vegetable oil, orange zest, fennel seeds, caraway seeds, aniseeds, cardamom, and salt. Let cool to lukewarm.

Pour the warm milk into a large bowl and sprinkle with the yeast. Let stand until foamy, about 5 minutes.

In another large bowl, whisk together 3½ cups of the all-purpose flour and all the rye flour. Stir 1 cup of the flour mixture into the yeast mixture with a wooden spoon. Beat in the lukewarm beer mixture and 1 cup molasses. Add the remaining flour mixture, 1 cup at a time. Knead the dough in the bowl, adding as much of the remaining 1 cup all-purpose flour as needed until the dough is no longer too sticky to be kneaded on a floured surface. Turn out the dough onto a lightly floured work surface and knead until smooth and elastic, about 10 minutes.

Transfer the dough to a buttered large bowl, cover with a kitchen towel, and let rise in a warm place until doubled in bulk, about 2 hours. Punch down the dough and divide it in half. Shape each half into a loaf, and place each loaf seam side down in a 9-by-5-inch loaf pan. Cover with a damp kitchen towel and let rise in a warm place until doubled in bulk, about 1½ hours.

Preheat oven to 375°F. Bake the loaves for 20 minutes. Meanwhile, in a bowl, stir together a little molasses with just enough water to make the mixture brushable. Brush the tops of the loaves with the molasses-water mixture and continue to bake until the loaves are dark golden brown and sound hollow when tapped on the bottom, about 25 minutes longer. Immediately turn the bread out of the pans, brush all over with more molasses-water mixture, and let cool completely on a wire rack. Store in zippered plastic bags until serving to keep the crusts soft. (The bread may be baked up to 1 day in advance and stored at room temperature, or up to 1 month in advance, frozen, and then thawed completely at room temperature before serving.) Cut the bread into thin slices just before serving.

MAKES 2 LOAVES

1 bottle (12 fl oz) dark beer or stout

½ cup unsalted butter or vegetable oil

3 tablespoons finely grated orange zest

1½ teaspoons ground fennel seeds

1½ teaspoons ground caraway seeds

1½ teaspoons ground aniseeds

¾ teaspoon ground cardamom

1 teaspoon salt

½ cup whole milk, warmed (105°–115°F)

5 teaspoons (2 packages) active dry yeast

4½ cups sifted all-purpose flour

3½ cups sifted medium rye flour

1 cup dark molasses, plus more for brushing

Beet and Apple Salad

8 beets, about 2 lb total weight

3 small red onions, unpeeled

3 tablespoons balsamic or red wine vinegar

2 tablespoons sunflower oil

Coarse salt and freshly ground pepper

4 Granny Smith apples, about 1½ lb total weight

1 tablespoon fresh lemon juice

½ cup crème fraîche or sour cream

12 curly red-leaf lettuce leaves

3 tablespoons pecan pieces, toasted
(see page 40)

You can use beets of a single color for this attractive salad, or you can combine red beets with a pink, golden, or even striped variety.

Preheat oven to 400°F. Trim the beet greens, leaving 1 inch of the stem intact. Scrub the beets and pat dry with paper towels. Wrap the beets and onions together in an aluminum foil packet, seal tightly, and place on a baking sheet. Roast the beets until they are tender when pierced with a fork, about 1¼ hours. When cool enough to handle, peel and trim the beets and onions, cut in half lengthwise, and then crosswise into thin slices. Transfer to a bowl. Add the vinegar, oil, ¼ teaspoon salt, and a pinch of pepper and stir until blended. Refrigerate, tightly covered, for at least 2 hours or up to 1 day.

Peel, halve, and core the apples, then cut into slices ¼ inch thick. Cut each slice into 3 pieces. Transfer to a bowl, add the lemon juice, and toss to coat. Add the crème fraîche or sour cream, ¼ teaspoon salt, and a pinch of pepper and stir until blended. Refrigerate, tightly covered, for at least 2 hours or up to 1 day.

To serve, arrange the lettuce leaves on a serving platter and top with separate mounds of the beet and the apple mixtures. Sprinkle with the pecans and serve.

MAKES 10–12 SERVINGS

Watercress and Radish Salad with Grapefruit

Here, pink grapefruits, which deliver a tart-sweet flavor, are paired with peppery green watercress and piquant red radishes in a colorful salad.

Working with 1 grapefruit at a time, cut a thin slice off the top and bottom, then stand it upright. Following the contour of the fruit, carefully cut from top to bottom to remove the peel and white pith. Holding the fruit over a bowl, cut along each side of the membranes between the sections, letting each freed section fall into the bowl. Repeat with the remaining 2 grapefruits, removing the seeds as you go. Drain away the juice and reserve for another use.

In a large, shallow serving bowl, whisk together the vinegar, mustard, and ½ teaspoon each salt and pepper. Add the olive oil in a slow, steady stream, whisking constantly until the dressing is emulsified. Add the grapefruit sections, top with the watercress, and then the radishes. Do not toss. Cover tightly with plastic wrap, add a layer of damp paper towels, and cover with another layer of wrap. Refrigerate for up to 4 hours before serving.

Just before serving, toss the salad to coat evenly with the dressing.

MAKES 10–12 SERVINGS

3 pink grapefruits

3 tablespoons red wine vinegar

1 tablespoon whole-grain mustard

Coarse salt and freshly ground pepper

6 tablespoons olive oil

4 bunches watercress, tough stems removed

6 large radishes, trimmed, halved lengthwise, and cut crosswise into thin slices

Kugelhopf

Kugelhopf, a fruit-and-nut-studded light yeast cake traditionally baked in a tall ring mold of the same name, is thought to have originated in Austria, although cooks in France, Germany, and elsewhere claim it as well.

½ cup warm water (105°–115°F)

¾ cup plus 1 teaspoon granulated sugar

5 teaspoons (2 packages) active dry yeast

1 cup unsalted butter, at room temperature

6 large eggs

1 tablespoon grated lemon zest

1 teaspoon salt

1 teaspoon vanilla extract

4 cups all-purpose flour, sifted

1 cup golden raisins

½ cup slivered blanched almonds, toasted (see page 40)

Confectioners' sugar, for dusting

In a small bowl, stir together the warm water and the 1 teaspoon of granulated sugar. Sprinkle with the yeast and let stand until foamy, about 5 minutes. In a large bowl, using an electric mixer on high speed, beat the butter and the ¾ cup sugar until light and fluffy. Beat in the eggs, one at a time. Beat in the lemon zest, salt, and vanilla. Add the yeast mixture and gradually beat in 2 cups of the flour. Beat on medium speed for 5 minutes. Gradually add the remaining flour and beat until the dough is elastic. Stir in the raisins.

Transfer the dough to a buttered large bowl, cover with a kitchen towel, and let rise in a warm place until doubled in bulk, 1½–2 hours. Punch down and stir in the almonds. On a floured surface, shape the dough into a 10-inch-long log. Transfer to a greased and floured 2½-qt kugelhopf or bundt pan, cover with a towel, and let rise in a warm place until the dough comes to within ½ inch of the rim, about 1 hour.

Preheat oven to 475°F. Bake for 10 minutes. Reduce oven temperature to 350°F, and bake until a toothpick inserted in the center comes out clean, 30–35 minutes. Let cool in the pan on a wire rack for 5 minutes. Turn out onto the rack to cool completely. Dust with confectioners' sugar, cut into slices, and serve.

MAKES 1 KUGELHOPF, OR 10–12 SERVINGS

Gingerbread with Lemon Cream

When dusting the gingerbreads with confectioners' sugar, use a doily or other stencil for a pretty design. Bake the gingerbreads up to a day in advance and store, tightly wrapped, at room temperature, then decorate just before serving.

1 cup apple juice or water, heated

½ cup dark molasses

2 tablespoons cider vinegar

3 cups all-purpose flour

1 cup firmly packed golden brown sugar

2 teaspoons ground ginger

2 teaspoons baking soda

½ teaspoon salt

⅔ cup sunflower oil

1½ cups heavy cream

3 tablespoons confectioners' sugar, plus more for dusting

1½ tablespoons grated lemon zest

Preheat oven to 350°F. Grease two 8-by-2-inch round cake pans. In a bowl, whisk together the apple juice or water, molasses, and vinegar. Sift together the flour, brown sugar, ground ginger, baking soda, and salt into a large bowl. Make a well in the center of the flour mixture. Pour in the oil and the molasses mixture and combine with a rubber spatula just until blended.

Divide the batter evenly between the prepared pans and smooth the tops. Bake until a toothpick inserted in the center comes out clean, about 30 minutes. Let cool completely in the pans on wire racks. Remove from the pans, transfer to 2 serving plates, and cover with plastic wrap if not serving immediately.

Up to 1 hour before serving, using an electric mixer on high speed, beat the cream until soft peaks form. Add the confectioners' sugar and lemon zest and beat just until stiff peaks form. Cover and refrigerate. Just before serving, dust the gingerbreads with confectioners' sugar, cut into wedges, and serve with a dollop of the lemon cream.

MAKES 2 GINGERBREADS, OR 10–12 SERVINGS

CHRISTMAS DAY OPEN HOUSE

Once the fun and frenzy of unwrapping gifts is over, a casual afternoon open house is a delightful way to extend the merriment of Christmas Day with neighbors, friends, and relatives. Your grateful guests—especially singles and families with kids—will be happy to have somewhere to go for mixing and mingling.

A bountiful holiday buffet, served in the dining room or kitchen, makes it easy to accommodate drop-ins throughout the day and into the evening. Set up a separate table for beverages, and welcome guests with a cup of homemade eggnog—with or without rum—followed by a steaming bowl of hot soup. Arrange multiple dining areas in the living room, with comfortable chairs grouped around low tables.

Use seasonal fruits, such as pomegranates, clustered with berries and fresh-picked greenery on white serving dishes and footed platters to create colorful decorating accents. Adorn the front hall with boughs and wreaths, and designate a bench or table for guests to leave hostess gifts. Set out gifts for them to take home as well, such as bags of homemade spiced nuts, tied with ribbons.

MENU

Eggnog

Sugar and Spice Pecans

Roasted Butternut Squash Soup

Herb-Rubbed Roast Turkey

*Cranberry, Onion,
and Ginger Conserve*

Braised Fennel Gratin

Wild Rice and Leek Salad

*Grapefruit, Endive, and
Pomegranate Salad*

Brown Sugar Pound Cake

Warm Winter Fruit Sauce

PLANNING AHEAD

2 WEEKS AHEAD

Prepare soup and freeze it

Toast pecans

Make cranberry conserve

1 DAY AHEAD

Brine turkey

Bake pound cake

Make croutons

Fill pecan bags

Prepare fruit sauce

3 HOURS AHEAD

Prepare wild rice salad

Braise fennel

Roast turkey

1 HOUR AHEAD

Make and chill eggnog

Make grapefruit salad, but do not dress

Bake gratin

JUST BEFORE SERVING

Add rum, whipped cream to eggnog

Carve turkey

Pecan Gift Bags

SUGAR AND SPICE PECANS • CELLOPHANE BAGS • RIBBON

These delicious pecans are an easy-to-make gift for guests at a holiday open house or similar affair. You can prepare the pecans 1–2 weeks in advance.

ONE Make the Sugar and Spice Pecans (page 99) and store in an airtight container.

TWO One day before the party, fill cellophane bags or other gift bags or small clear plastic boxes with the pecans, putting a few scoopfuls in each container.

THREE Adorn each bag with a festive holiday bow. Place the bags in a basket or on a platter near the front door. Invite guests to take one home.

Eggnog

This eggnog is made like a custard, cooked over heat until it is perfectly smooth and the consistancy of softly whipped cream. To guard against overcooking, use an instant-read thermometer to judge when the custard is ready.

In a large, heavy saucepan, whisk together the egg yolks, the ¾ cup sugar, the 1 teaspoon nutmeg, and citrus zests. Stir in the milk and 2 cups of the cream. Place over low heat and cook, stirring constantly with a rubber spatula, just until the mixture thickens enough to coat the spatula and a finger run along its length leaves a track, or an instant-read thermometer reads 160°F, about 20 minutes.

Immediately remove from the heat and strain through a sieve into a pitcher or bowl. Cover and refrigerate to chill thoroughly, about 1 hour.

Just before serving, in a bowl, whip the remaining 1 cup cream with the 2 tablespoons sugar until soft peaks form. Pour the chilled custard into a punch bowl and stir in the liquor, if using. Dollop the whipped cream on top and sprinkle with nutmeg.

MAKES ABOUT 8 CUPS, OR 10–12 SERVINGS

12 large egg yolks

¾ cup plus 2 tablespoons sugar

1 teaspoon freshly grated nutmeg, plus more for garnish

Grated zest of 1 orange

Grated zest of 1 lemon

2 cups whole milk

3 cups heavy cream

½–¾ cup dark rum, cognac, or bourbon (optional)

Sugar and Spice Pecans

Lightly sweetened and richly spiced pecans are simple to make, yet difficult to stop eating. If you grind the whole spices yourself, these nuts will be particularly flavorful. If not, make sure the ground spices have spent no more than a few months in your cupboard. Serve in small bowls and make extra to pack into gift bags for your guests.

Preheat oven to 350°F. Spread the nuts on a rimmed baking sheet and toast, stirring the nuts once or twice, until lightly browned, about 10 minutes. Remove from oven.

Heat a large, heavy frying pan over medium-high heat until very hot. Add the oil and nuts and stir to coat evenly. Sprinkle with the sugar, 1 teaspoon salt, cinnamon, cumin, allspice, and cayenne and cook, stirring constantly, until the sugar melts over the nuts and caramelizes, 1–2 minutes. (If the nuts start to burn, reduce the heat slightly.) Return the nuts to the rimmed baking sheet, spreading them evenly, and let cool. Serve warm or at room temperature. Store in an airtight container for up to 2 weeks.

MAKES 4 CUPS, OR 10–12 SERVINGS

4 cups pecan halves

2 teaspoons grapeseed oil or peanut oil

5 tablespoons firmly packed turbinado sugar or golden brown sugar

Coarse salt

½ teaspoon ground cinnamon

¼ teaspoon ground cumin

¼ teaspoon ground allspice

¼ teaspoon cayenne pepper, or more to taste

Roasted Butternut Squash Soup

2 butternut squashes, 5–6 lb total weight

6 tablespoons unsalted butter

Coarse salt and freshly ground black pepper

1 head garlic, cloves separated but unpeeled

4 fresh thyme sprigs

4 fresh rosemary sprigs

1 cup chopped shallots

¾ cup dry white wine

4 cups chicken or vegetable broth

1 cup heavy cream

1 teaspoon freshly grated nutmeg

⅛ teaspoon cayenne pepper

ROSEMARY CROUTONS

10 slices coarse country bread, ½ inch thick

4 tablespoons unsalted butter, melted

2 fresh rosemary sprigs

Coarse salt and freshly ground black pepper

Roasting winter squashes intensifies their flavor and sweetness, creating a perfect base for this simple soup. Butternut squash is a good choice, but acorn or delicata can be used in its place. You can make the soup 2 weeks in advance, freeze it, and reheat it slowly over low heat without thawing. If it is too thick, add a little broth or water. The croutons can hold for a day or two at room temperature in a zippered plastic bag.

Preheat oven to 375°F. Cut the squashes in half lengthwise and scoop out the seeds with a spoon. Melt 2 tablespoons of the butter, and brush the butter on the cut surfaces. Sprinkle the cut surfaces with ½ teaspoon each salt and black pepper. Stuff the cavities with the garlic cloves and 1 sprig each of the thyme and rosemary. Then carefully turn the squash halves cut side down on a rimmed baking sheet. Bake until very tender when pierced with a knife, 45–50 minutes. Set aside to cool.

While the squashes are baking, make the croutons: Cut the bread into ½-inch cubes and transfer to a large bowl. Add the melted butter, rosemary sprigs, ½ teaspoon salt, and ¼ teaspoon black pepper and stir to mix. Spread on a large, rimmed baking sheet and bake until browned and crisp, 15–18 minutes. Discard the rosemary.

When the squash halves are cool, scoop the flesh out into a bowl. Squeeze the roasted garlic from its skin into the same bowl. In a large soup pot over medium-high heat, melt the remaining 4 tablespoons butter. Add the shallots and cook, stirring frequently, until softened, 3–4 minutes. Add the squash and garlic to the pot and, using the back of a spoon, mash all the ingredients together. Pour in the wine and broth, stir to mix, and bring to a simmer over medium-high heat. Stir in the cream. Remove from the heat and using an immersion blender, purée the soup in the pot. Alternatively, purée in batches in a stand blender and return the soup to the pot.

Add the nutmeg, cayenne, 1 tablespoon plus 2 teaspoons salt, and ¼ teaspoon black pepper and heat to serving temperature. Taste and adjust the seasoning.

Pour the soup into a warmed tureen. To serve, ladle into individual warmed bowls and float a few croutons on top.

MAKES 10–12 SERVINGS

Herb-Rubbed Roast Turkey

Home cooks everywhere are discovering that immersing the holiday turkey in brine the night before roasting adds flavor and juiciness to this traditional Christmas dinner centerpiece. For this recipe, the bird is then roasted in a very hot oven that guarantees crisp, golden brown skin, moist flesh, and a surprisingly short cooking time of just 2 hours.

Remove the neck and giblets from the cavity, wrap in plastic, and refrigerate while brining.

Place the turkey in a pot or clean bucket large enough to hold it. Rub the 2 cups salt all over the bird. Add 8 qt water and stir until the salt dissolves. Place in the refrigerator for 10–12 hours. Remove the turkey from the brine and rinse the cavity and skin under cold running water for several minutes.

In a small bowl, combine the butter, chopped parsley, chopped thyme, sage, rosemary, 1 teaspoon salt, and ½ teaspoon pepper. Mash with a wooden spoon until well blended. Using your fingers, gently loosen the skin from the turkey breast and smear half of the butter mixture under the skin. Let stand at room temperature for 1 hour.

Meanwhile, cut the reserved giblets into 1-inch pieces, keeping the liver pieces separate. In a large saucepan, combine the neck and giblets (minus the liver); garlic cloves; half of the chopped onions, carrots, and celery; the bay leaf; parsley stems; thyme sprigs; and ½ teaspoon salt. Add 3 qt water and bring to a boil. Reduce the heat to a simmer and cook for 2 hours. Add the liver and cook for 5 minutes longer. Strain the stock, discarding the vegetables, neck, and giblets, and refrigerate. You should have 3 cups; if not, add up to 1 cup water.

Preheat oven to 450°F. Place half of the remaining onions, carrots, and celery in the turkey cavity along with 1 tablespoon of the remaining herb butter. Tie the legs together with kitchen string and tuck the first joint of each wing under the second joint to prevent overbrowning. Set the turkey, breast side down, on a V-shaped rack in a shallow roasting pan. Scatter the remaining vegetables over the pan bottom, and pour in 1 cup water. Rub the bottom of the bird with half of the remaining herb butter. Roast for 1 hour, then, with a kitchen towel in each hand, turn the turkey breast side up. Pour 1 cup water into the pan and rub the breast skin with the remaining herb butter. Reduce oven temperature to 425°F and roast for 30 minutes longer. Add 1 cup water to the pan. (If the skin is looking overly browned, cover loosely with foil.) Roast until the breast is nicely browned and an instant-read thermometer inserted into the thickest part of the thigh away from the bone reads 175°F, 30–40 minutes longer. Transfer the turkey to a platter and let rest for 20–30 minutes.

Remove the rack and reserve the juices, leaving ⅓ cup in the bottom of the roasting pan. Place the pan over 2 burners on the stove top over medium heat. Add the flour and cook, stirring constantly with a wooden spoon, until the flour turns nut brown, about 3 minutes. Pour in the wine and cook, scraping up the browned bits from the pan bottom. Pour in the remaining reserved stock and pan juices and bring to a boil. Reduce the heat to a simmer until the gravy has thickened slightly, 5–8 minutes. Season to taste with salt and pepper.

Carve the turkey and serve with the gravy.

MAKES 10–12 SERVINGS

1 turkey, 12–14 lb, thawed in the refrigerator if frozen

2 cups coarse salt, plus more for seasoning

½ cup unsalted butter, at room temperature

2 tablespoons chopped fresh flat-leaf parsley, plus 6 stems

2 tablespoons chopped fresh thyme, plus 3 sprigs

1 tablespoon chopped fresh sage

1 tablespoon chopped fresh rosemary

Freshly ground pepper

3 cloves garlic

4 yellow onions, chopped

4 carrots, chopped

4 celery stalks, chopped

1 bay leaf

⅓ cup all-purpose flour

1 cup light red wine, such as Beaujolais, or white wine

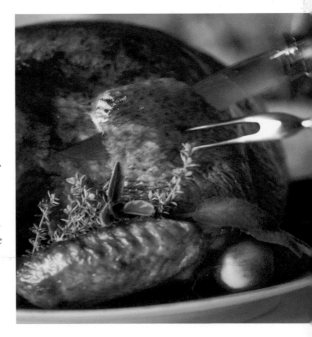

Cranberry, Onion, and Ginger Conserve

The flavors of this conserve deepen and meld over time, so make it at least 3 days (or up to 2 weeks) ahead and refrigerate it. Bring to room temperature before serving.

In a large frying pan, melt the butter over medium-high heat. Add the onion and cook, stirring frequently, until softened, 3–4 minutes. Add the cranberries, apples, raisins, brown sugar, ginger, vinegar, cranberry or apple juice, cinnamon, ⅛ teaspoon salt, and ½ teaspoon pepper and stir to combine. Bring to a boil over high heat. Reduce the heat to a simmer and cook until the cranberries and apples are soft, about 15 minutes. Transfer to a bowl and let cool completely, then cover and refrigerate. Remove from the refrigerator at least 20 minutes before serving.

MAKES ABOUT 5 CUPS, OR 10–12 SERVINGS

2 tablespoons unsalted butter

1 cup finely chopped red onion

1 bag (12 oz) fresh cranberries

2 large Granny Smith apples, peeled, cored, and coarsely chopped

1 cup golden raisins

1⅓ cups firmly packed dark brown sugar

2 tablespoons finely chopped, peeled fresh ginger

¼ cup cider vinegar

1 cup cranberry juice or apple juice

½ teaspoon ground cinnamon

Coarse salt and freshly ground pepper

Braised Fennel Gratin

Plump fennel bulbs have the most flavor, so when shopping for fennel, choose bulbs that are smooth, rounded, and fat and have lots of feathery tops. You can braise the fennel and assemble the gratin a few hours ahead, refrigerate it, and then put it in the oven when the turkey comes out.

Cut off the stems and feathery tops and any bruised outer stalks from the fennel bulbs and quarter the bulbs lengthwise. Chop 2 tablespoons of the tops and reserve for garnish.

Preheat oven to 425°F. Divide the olive oil evenly between 2 large frying pans and place over medium-high heat. Divide the fennel between the pans and sprinkle each batch with ½ teaspoon each salt and pepper. Sauté, turning occasionally with tongs, until softened and lightly browned, 5–7 minutes. Divide the thyme sprigs, wine, and broth evenly between the 2 pans and bring to a boil. Reduce the heat to a simmer, cover, and cook until the fennel is very tender, about 20 minutes. Using the tongs, transfer the fennel to 1 or 2 gratin dishes or other baking dish large enough to hold the fennel in a single layer.

Pour the cooking liquid and thyme from 1 frying pan into the other. Add the cream, bring to a boil over high heat, and reduce the sauce to about ½ cup, 3–4 minutes. Discard the thyme sprigs and pour the sauce over the fennel. Sprinkle the fennel evenly with the Parmesan. Bake until the cheese is melted, 10–15 minutes. Sprinkle with the reserved fennel tops and serve.

MAKES 10–12 SERVINGS

8 large fennel bulbs

6 tablespoons extra-virgin olive oil

Coarse salt and freshly ground pepper

8 fresh thyme sprigs

½ cup dry white wine

1½ cups chicken broth

¼ cup heavy cream

½ cup grated Parmesan cheese

Wild Rice and Leek Salad

For the fullest flavors, make the salad in the morning and let it stand for several hours at room temperature before serving. Be sure that the zucchini are small and fresh; they turn bitter if stored for more than 2 or 3 days.

In a large saucepan over high heat, combine 2 pieces of the dark green leek tops, the wild rice, 3 cups water, and 1½ teaspoons salt. Bring to a boil, stir once, reduce the heat to low, cover, and simmer until the water is absorbed and the wild rice is fluffy and tender, 35–55 minutes. Remove from the heat and let stand, covered, for 10 minutes. Discard the leek greens and drain out any excess water. Transfer to a large serving bowl.

While the wild rice is cooking, in another large saucepan over high heat, combine the brown rice, 2 cups water, 2 more leek tops, and 1 teaspoon salt. Bring to a boil, reduce the heat to low, cover, and simmer until the water is absorbed and the brown rice is fluffy and tender, 35–45 minutes. Remove from the heat and let stand, covered, for 10 minutes. Discard the leek greens and add the brown rice along with the currants to the bowl holding the wild rice.

In a large frying pan over medium-high heat, warm ⅓ cup of the olive oil. Add the sliced leeks and ½ teaspoon salt and cook until tender, 4–5 minutes. Transfer to the bowl holding the rices. Heat the remaining olive oil in the same pan over high heat. Add the zucchini and cook until tender-crisp, 8–10 minutes. Stir in the parsley, cumin, allspice, coriander, cayenne, ¾ teaspoon salt, ½ teaspoon black pepper, and lemon juice. Transfer to the bowl holding the rices, add the almonds, and mix gently. Taste and adjust the seasoning. Serve warm or at room temperature.

MAKES 10–12 SERVINGS

2 large leeks, dark green leaf tops reserved, white and light green parts thinly sliced

1½ cups wild rice, rinsed until water runs clear

Coarse salt

1 cup brown rice

1 cup dried currants

⅔ cup extra-virgin olive oil

1 lb slender zucchini, trimmed and cut into ½-inch chunks

½ cup chopped fresh flat-leaf parsley

2 teaspoons ground cumin

1 teaspoon ground allspice

1 teaspoon ground coriander

¼ teaspoon cayenne pepper

Freshly ground black pepper

¼ cup fresh lemon juice

¾ cup slivered blanched almonds, toasted (see page 40)

Grapefruit, Endive, and Pomegranate Salad

Grapefruit, like most citrus fruits, tastes best in the winter. Here, it is used in a refreshing salad that is ideally served after the main course, to clear the palate for dessert. The greens will wilt the moment they are tossed with the dressing; if you prefer, serve the dressing on the side.

In a large serving bowl, toss together the lettuce, watercress, and endive.

Cut a slice off the top and bottom of 1 grapefruit, then stand it upright. Following the contour of the fruit, slice off the peel and white pith in thick strips. Holding the fruit over a bowl, carefully cut along each side of the membranes between the sections, letting each freed section and any juice fall into the bowl. Squeeze additional juice from the membrane into the bowl. Repeat with the remaining 2 grapefruits, removing the seeds as you go. Using a slotted spoon, transfer the sections to the serving bowl, scattering them over the greens.

In a food processor or blender, combine 2 tablespoons of the grapefruit juice, the orange juice, citrus oil, vinegar, shallots, olive oil, and ¼ teaspoon each salt and pepper. Process until smooth and well blended. Taste and adjust the seasoning. Pour the dressing over the salad. Add the pomegranate seeds, toss, and serve at once.

MAKES 10–12 SERVINGS

3 heads butter or Bibb lettuce, leaves separated and torn into large pieces

2 bunches watercress, tough stems removed

3 heads Belgian endive, cored and separated into leaves

3 pink grapefruits

1 tablespoon fresh orange juice

⅛ teaspoon lemon or orange oil

2 tablespoons balsamic vinegar

3 tablespoons minced shallots

6 tablespoons extra-virgin olive oil

Coarse salt and freshly ground pepper

½ cup pomegranate seeds

Brown Sugar Pound Cake

This buttery pound cake gets its pleasant crunch from cornmeal and its rich aroma from brown sugar. You can make the cake the day before serving and store it at room temperature, or up to a month in advance, put it in waxed paper and a zippered plastic bag, and freeze it.

Preheat oven to 350°F. Grease and flour one 10-inch tube pan or bundt pan or two 4½-by-8½ inch loaf pans. In a bowl, sift together the flour, cornmeal, baking soda, and salt. (If any cornmeal remains in the sifter, just stir it in.) In a small bowl, combine the sour cream and vanilla and almond extracts.

In a large bowl, using an electric mixer on medium speed, beat the butter until creamy. Add the brown sugar and beat on high speed until lightened, 4–5 minutes. Add the egg yolks, one at a time, beating well after each addition. Reduce the speed to low and add the cornmeal mixture in 3 batches, alternating with the sour cream mixture in 2 batches, beginning and ending with the cornmeal mixture.

In another bowl, with spotlessly clean beaters, beat the egg whites and cream of tartar on medium speed until soft peaks form. Gradually add the granulated sugar and beat until the peaks are stiff but not dry. Stir one-third of the egg whites into the batter to lighten it, then, using a rubber spatula, gently fold in the remaining whites. Scrape the batter into the prepared pan(s) and spread evenly. Bake until a toothpick inserted in the center comes out clean, 70–80 minutes. Let cool in the pan(s) for 10 minutes, then slide a thin knife around the edges to loosen. Invert the cake(s) on a wire rack, turn right side up, and let cool completely. Dust with confectioners' sugar before serving.

MAKES 10–12 SERVINGS

2 cups sifted all-purpose flour

1 cup cornmeal

¼ teaspoon baking soda

¼ teaspoon salt

1 cup sour cream

1½ teaspoons vanilla extract

½ teaspoon almond extract

1 cup unsalted butter, at room temperature

2 cups firmly packed golden brown sugar

6 large eggs, separated, at room temperature

¼ teaspoon cream of tartar

½ cup granulated sugar

Confectioners' sugar for dusting

Warm Winter Fruit Sauce

Serve spoonfuls of this sauce with each wedge of pound cake. This sauce is also good on vanilla ice cream. Pear nectar can be used in place of the wine.

In a large frying pan over medium-high heat, melt the butter. Add the pears, brown sugar, and vanilla bean pods and seeds and cook, stirring occasionally, until the pears are almost tender, about 5 minutes. Stir in the dried fruits and wine and bring to a simmer. Reduce the heat to maintain a simmer and continue to cook until all the fruits are tender and plumped and the sauce is thickened, about 15 minutes longer. Remove and discard the vanilla bean pods. Serve the sauce warm, or let cool, cover, and refrigerate for up to 1 day. Then reheat gently before serving.

MAKES ABOUT 6 CUPS, OR 10–12 SERVINGS

2 tablespoons unsalted butter

5 firm but ripe pears, about 2½ lb total weight, peeled, cored, and coarsely chopped

¼ cup firmly packed golden brown sugar

1 vanilla bean, split lengthwise, seeds scraped out and seeds and pods reserved

1 cup dried peaches, coarsely chopped

1 cup dried pears, coarsely chopped

½ cup dried cranberries

½ cup prunes, pitted and halved

1½ cups Gewürztraminer or Riesling

WINE COUNTRY CHRISTMAS DINNER

Christmas entertaining in California's wine country means informal elegance and menus that pair fresh seasonal ingredients with the best local wines. That same blend of celebratory and casual elements can strike just the right note for a luxurious Christmas dinner at your house, inspired by the pleasures of wine and the bounties of winter, like Dungeness crab, tenderloin of beef, Meyer lemons, and Bartlett pears.

A wine-red table runner adds a striking holiday accent to the warmth of a wood dining table. Round out the look with silver, crystal, and china, accented with homespun, natural decorations, such as olive branches, roses, clusters of grapes, and fanciful place cards made with pears or pomegranates. A silver bowl filled with winter fruits and sprigs of greenery and a holiday wreath festooned with red and yellow crab apples and berries add inviting splashes of color to the room.

Serve the crab salad as a plated appetizer, then set out the rest of the meal buffet style on the sideboard. After dessert, serve the cheese tray and a final glass of wine in the living room, followed by the truffles, with coffee and after-dinner drinks.

MENU

Dungeness Crab with
Meyer Lemon Cream

Mesclun Salad with Vinaigrette

Roast Tenderloin of Beef
with Cabernet Sauvignon Sauce

Potato-Parsnip Gratin

Leaves of Brussels Sprouts with
Hazelnut Beurre Noisette

Bartlett Pears Roasted with
Late-Harvest Riesling

Chocolate Truffles

PLANNING AHEAD

3 DAYS AHEAD
Make truffles
Prepare lemon cream

1 DAY AHEAD
Purchase flowers, olive sprigs
Make pear place names
Prepare Brussels sprouts

2 HOURS AHEAD
Make gratin
Arrange cheese tray
Roast pears
Prepare and cook tenderloin

JUST BEFORE SERVING
Drizzle crab with lemon cream
Toss salad

Pear Place Names

PEARS • CARD STOCK • PEN • STRING OR RIBBON

Put one of these festive pears, each outfitted with a simple, yet elegant place card, above each guest's plate.

ONE Gather all the supplies you will need: firm, unblemished pears (apples or pomegranates will also work) with stems intact; heavy paper or card stock in a color that complements your table decorations; metallic or other pretty string; and a gold, silver, or glitter pen.

TWO Cut the paper into long, narrow strips or the shape of your choice. Write the name of each guest on a separate strip of paper.

THREE Make a small hole in the top of each strip of paper with a straight pin. Thread a length of string through the hole, and tie a small knot near the tag so it will stay in place. Loosely tie the string around the pear stem and make a bow.

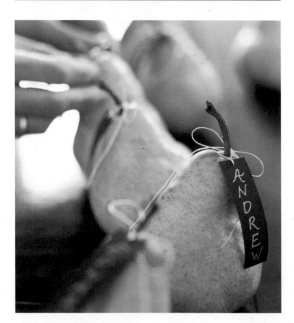

Dungeness Crab with Meyer Lemon Cream

3 Dungeness crabs, about 1½ lb each, cooked and cleaned

32–40 whole fresh chives, plus ½ cup finely snipped fresh chives, for garnish

MEYER LEMON CREAM

2 large egg yolks

2 teaspoons Dijon mustard

Grated zest of 6 Meyer lemons

Coarse salt

2 cups sunflower oil

¼ cup crème fraîche

Juice of 2 Meyer lemons

Sweet and succulent, Dungeness crabmeat makes a wonderful holiday dish. Here, it is paired with another favorite wintertime ingredient, fragrant Meyer lemons. Look for them in farmers' markets and specialty produce stores.

Carefully remove the crab claws and legs from the body. Crack the claws and legs and set aside. Remove the crabmeat from the body, picking over and discarding any cartilage and shell bits. Set the crabmeat aside.

To make the lemon cream, in a small, high-sided bowl, whisk together the egg yolks, mustard, lemon zest, and a pinch of salt. Begin whisking in the oil, a few drops at a time. Once the mixture becomes thicker and lighter yellow, add the oil in a more constant, yet still slow stream. If at any time the mixture looks as if it is beginning to curdle, stop adding the oil and whisk vigorously until the emulsion returns before proceeding. Continue until all the oil has been whisked into the egg yolks. Whisk in the crème fraîche, followed by the lemon juice. (The lemon cream will keep at this point, covered and refrigerated, for up to 3 days.)

To serve, place 4 chives on each individual plate, arranging them in a square. Divide the crabmeat from the body evenly among the plates, packing it into a compact mound. Drizzle with the lemon cream and sprinkle with the chopped chives. Serve immediately. Serve the cracked crab claws and crab legs on the side.

MAKES 8–10 SERVINGS

Mesclun Salad with Vinaigrette

VINAIGRETTE

2 tablespoons balsamic vinegar

2 teaspoons minced shallots

1 teaspoon Dijon mustard

¼ teaspoon coarse salt

½ cup extra-virgin olive oil

1–1¼ lb mesclun, carefully washed and dried

Coarse salt and freshly ground pepper

A simple salad of mesclun, a mix of tender, young lettuces, greens, and herbs, is a welcome antidote to the typically rich dishes of a celebratory dinner. The use of balsamic vinegar in the vinaigrette adds a pleasant touch of sweetness. For a photo of the finished recipe, see page 112.

To make the vinaigrette, in the bottom of a large salad bowl, whisk together the vinegar, shallots, mustard, and ¼ teaspoon salt. Slowly whisk in the oil to form an emulsion.

Add the mesclun to the bowl and toss gently to coat evenly. Season to taste with salt and pepper. Serve at once.

MAKES 8–10 SERVINGS

Roast Tenderloin of Beef with Cabernet Sauvignon Sauce

2 center-cut pieces beef tenderloin, about 2 lb each

Coarse salt and freshly ground pepper

2 tablespoons unsalted butter

2 tablespoons sunflower oil

Fresh herb sprigs, such as thyme and sage, for garnish

CABERNET SAUVIGNON SAUCE

6 shallots, chopped

2 cups Cabernet Sauvignon

½ cup veal *demi-glace*

1 teaspoon red currant jelly

Coarse salt and freshly ground pepper

2 tablespoons unsalted butter (optional)

For special occasions, French cooks prepare the legendary châteaubriand, which calls for a thick slice of beef cut from the center of the tenderloin, grilled, and served with a butter sauce. This recipe uses the same tender, mild-flavored cut, but pairs it with a full-bodied red wine sauce. Make sure your butcher gives you the choice center cut, as many shops sell top sirloin as châteaubriand.

Preheat oven to 425°F. To prepare the beef, trim off any fat and remove any silver skin. Season generously with salt and pepper.

In a large, heavy ovenproof pan, melt the butter with the oil over high heat. Add the tenderloins and sear until well browned on all sides, 10–15 minutes. Transfer the pan to the oven. Roast the beef until an instant-read thermometer reads 130°F for medium-rare, about 15 minutes. Transfer the tenderloins to a cutting board, cover loosely with aluminum foil, and let rest for 15 minutes.

To make the sauce, in the same pan over medium heat, sauté the shallots until translucent, about 5 minutes. Add the wine and 1 cup water, raise the heat to high, and bring to a boil. Cook, stirring to scrape up any browned bits from the pan bottom, until the liquid is reduced by half, about 5 minutes. Add the *demi-glace*, reduce the heat to medium-high, and cook, stirring occasionally, for 5 minutes. Strain the sauce through a fine-mesh sieve into a saucepan. Stir in the jelly and season to taste with salt and pepper. Keep the sauce warm over low heat. Just before serving, whisk in the butter, if desired.

To serve, slice the beef and arrange 2 slices on each plate. Spoon the sauce over the meat and garnish with sprigs of herbs.

MAKES 10–12 SERVINGS

Potato-Parsnip Gratin

Here, the rich and velvety classic combination of potatoes and cream is enhanced by the addition of layers of thinly sliced ivory parsnips. Look for firm, blemish-free parsnips, and remove the woody core before slicing.

4 tablespoons unsalted butter, at room temperature

1 clove garlic, pressed or finely mashed in a mortar

2 lb Yukon gold potatoes, peeled and sliced ¼ inch thick

1 lb parsnips, peeled and sliced ¼ inch thick

Coarse salt and freshly ground pepper

2 cups heavy cream

Preheat oven to 350°F. In a small bowl, mash together the butter and garlic. Rub a 9-by-13-inch oval gratin dish with 1 tablespoon of the garlic butter. Layer one-third of the potato slices, slightly overlapping, over the bottom of the dish (reserve the best-looking slices for the top layer). Cover with half of the parsnip slices. Sprinkle ½ teaspoon salt and a few grinds of pepper evenly over the parsnips. Repeat the layers using half of the remaining potato slices and all of the remaining parsnip slices, and again sprinkling with salt and pepper. Top with the remaining potato slices and sprinkle with ½ teaspoon salt and a few grinds of pepper. Carefully pour the cream evenly over the layers. Dot the top with the remaining garlic butter. Place the dish on a baking sheet.

Bake the potatoes until tender when pierced with the tip of a knife and the top is a golden brown, about 1½ hours. Let stand for 10 minutes, then serve hot.

MAKES 8–10 SERVINGS

Leaves of Brussels Sprouts with Hazelnut Beurre Noisette

Light and crispy, this presentation appeals to many who would otherwise not try Brussels sprouts. Do not be afraid to cook the butter to a golden brown. You'll reap the benefits of the extra minute in the nutty flavor that it adds to the dish.

1½ lb Brussels sprouts

½ cup unsalted butter

½ cup chopped hazelnuts

Coarse salt and freshly ground pepper

Lemon wedges, for garnish

To separate the leaves from the sprouts, trim off the stem end of each sprout and peel off the leaves. If this becomes difficult near the center, place them in ice water for 1 hour, drain, and continue peeling. Cut the innermost, tightly packed leaves into quarters.

Bring a large pot three-fourths full of salted water to a boil over high heat. Add the quartered innermost leaves and cook for 2 minutes. Add the remaining leaves and cook for 1 minute longer. Drain the leaves, plunge into ice water to refresh, and drain again. Spread out the leaves on a dry kitchen towel and pat gently to remove all water, or gently spin dry in a salad spinner. (The Brussels sprouts can be prepared up to this point the day before and stored, wrapped in damp paper towels in a plastic bag, in the refrigerator.)

In a large sauté pan over medium-high heat, melt the butter. Add the hazelnuts and cook until the butter has browned and the hazelnuts are fragrant and golden brown, about 3 minutes. Add the Brussels sprouts leaves and cook, tossing to coat with the butter, until heated through, about 2 minutes. Season to taste with salt and pepper. Transfer to a warmed serving dish, garnish with the lemon wedges, and serve immediately.

MAKES 8–10 SERVINGS

Bartlett Pears Roasted
with Late-Harvest Riesling

3 cups late-harvest Riesling

1 vanilla bean

8 firm but ripe Bartlett pears with stems intact

Juice of 2 lemons

Sugar, for coating

Heavy cream or crème fraîche, for serving

Fresh mint sprigs and raspberries, for garnish

Late-harvest wines are made from grapes that have been left on the vines until the final days of the harvest. They are particularly sweet and usually have a high alcohol content. The wine in this recipe mingles with the pears and their juices and the subtle perfume of vanilla bean to make an ambrosial nectar.

Preheat oven to 400°F. Pour the wine into the bottom of a light-colored gratin dish just large enough to hold the pears upright. Using a paring knife, cut the vanilla bean in half lengthwise and, using the tip of the knife, scrape out the seeds. Add both the pods and the seeds to the wine.

Leaving the top stem intact, peel each pear, then cut a thin slice off the bottom so that it will stand upright. Core the pears from the bottom, rub them with lemon juice, and roll in sugar to coat. Place the pears upright in the gratin dish.

Roast the pears, basting frequently, until tender and golden, 40–60 minutes, depending on their ripeness. The tip of a knife should easily pierce the flesh.

Serve hot, warm, or cold with the wine syrup from the dish, a spoonful of cream or crème fraîche, and a mint sprig.

MAKES 8 SERVINGS

Chocolate Truffles

Use only the highest-quality chocolate for making these truffles. Check the packaging for the cacao content, which indicates how much of the product is made up of ground cacao, rather than sugar. The higher the percentage, the better the chocolate. The truffles can be made up to 2 weeks in advance and stored, tightly covered, in the refrigerator.

In a saucepan over medium heat, bring the cream to a boil. Remove from the heat and add the chopped chocolate all at once, then stir continuously until it is fully melted, smooth, and shiny. Beat in the butter until smooth. Pour into a bowl and stir in the liqueur. Refrigerate until set, about 1 hour.

Line a baking sheet with parchment paper. Using a spoon, scoop out 1-inch balls onto the prepared baking sheet. Refrigerate until chilled, about 30 minutes.

To shape the truffles, roll each ball between your palms until it is perfectly round. Sift the cocoa powder into a shallow bowl. Roll the balls in the cocoa powder until evenly coated. Serve at room temperature arranged on a tray or in decorative paper candy cups.

MAKES ABOUT 3 DOZEN TRUFFLES

2 cups heavy cream

1 lb bittersweet or semisweet chocolate, finely chopped

½ cup unsalted butter, at room temperature

½ cup cognac, Grand Marnier, or other liqueur

1 cup unsweetened cocoa powder

A HOLIDAY CHEESE TRAY

Cheese is a wonderful addition to a special Christmas feast. The color, texture, shape, and size of cheeses vary enormously. The type of milk used—cow, goat, sheep, or a combination—helps determine the overall personality of any cheese. When assembling a cheese tray, aim for variety, planning on three or four different types. For the holidays, try a blue cheese, such as Stilton or Gorgonzola; a soft-ripened Brie or Saint-André; a pressed, aged sheep's milk cheese like Manchego; and a tangy chèvre, such as Montrachet. Arrange the cheeses on a silver tray or platter garnished with grape leaves or fresh herbs. Serve with thinly sliced bread, fresh fruit such as grapes or figs, and wine. Cabernet Sauvignon, Pinot Noir, Sauvignon Blanc, and Chardonnay all marry well with this assortment.

NEW YEAR'S EVE IN THE CITY

From the Champagne to the conversation, everything about New Year's Eve should sparkle—especially when you're hosting a big, urban-chic party. Set an elegant, modern mood with the glitter of silver—trays and platters for the hors d'oeuvres, a gleaming pedestal for vintage Champagne flutes, and dishes filled with silver-coated almonds. Create floral displays for the mantel and serving tables by arranging white star lilies in glass vases filled with silver Christmas ornaments.

Stock the bar with iced Champagne (figuring one bottle for every few wine drinkers), sparkling cider or ginger ale, and plenty of sparkling water—the only beverages you need to complement the flavors of the festive finger-food menu. Almost everything can be prepared ahead of time, with the room-temperature foods arranged at a few buffet stations and warm items passed by you and a helpful friend or two throughout the evening. Set up a separate table for the desserts right from the start, so guests can indulge in the full array of nibbling options whenever they arrive. As midnight approaches, circulate with Champagne, and hand out sparklers for a dazzling toast to a bright New Year.

MENU

Crab, Fennel, and Truffle Oil
Salad in Radicchio Cups

Cremini Mushrooms Stuffed with
Creamy Spinach and Quail Eggs

Thyme-Roasted Short Ribs
with Orange Gremolata

Chard Fritters with Yogurt-
Garlic-Chive Dipping Sauce

Polenta Crostini Topped
with Smoked Trout, Apple,
and Walnut Salad

Belgian Endive Spears
Topped with Goat Cheese
and Chopped Pistachios

Lemon-Lime Tartlets

Fallen Chocolate Cake with
Chocolate Shavings

PLANNING AHEAD

NIGHT BEFORE PARTY

Simmer ribs and refrigerate

Cook polenta

Chill Champagne

Prepare tartlet dough

Arrange flowers

4 HOURS AHEAD

Make yogurt sauce, prepare chard

Prepare filling and bake shells for tartlets

Mix chocolate cake batter

Prepare crab salad

2 HOURS AHEAD

Prepare *gremolata*

Make and assemble endive hors d'oeuvres

Fill radicchio cups

Lilies and Silver Balls

CLEAR VASES • SILVER ORNAMENTS • WHITE LILIES

Remarkably simple, these flower arrangements add a glittery and reflective shine to any table or mantel on New Year's Eve. You can use vases of different heights, and any white flower will look stunning displayed with shiny ornaments.

ONE Carefully take off the silver top of each ornament so that the ornament will fill with water. Arrange the ornaments in layers in each vase, filling the vases about half full and mixing big and small ornaments.

TWO Slowly pour water into each vase, allowing the ornaments to fill with liquid and gradually sink to the bottom of the vase.

THREE Measure the height of the flowers alongside the vase and cut the stems accordingly. For a cascading look, trim the stems at an angle so the blossoms hover just over the edge of the vase. Arrange each stem by sticking it between the ornaments for support. Add additional water as needed to cover the stems with plenty of liquid.

Crab, Fennel, and Truffle Oil Salad in Radicchio Cups

Sometimes a head of radicchio is so firmly packed that it is difficult to separate whole leaves to use as cups. But any portion of a leaf will do, as long as it has a nice concave shape that will neatly hold a small nest of salad.

In a bowl, combine the fennel, crabmeat, shallots, celery, chives, and parsley. Add the truffle oil, lemon juice, mayonnaise, ½ teaspoon salt, and a few grinds of pepper. Gently mix with a fork until evenly blended; do not break up the lumps of crabmeat. Taste and adjust the seasoning. If desired, cover and refrigerate for up to 4 hours.

Remove and discard any blemished leaves from each head of radicchio. Separate the largest outer leaves, keeping them as intact as possible. You should have about 40 cupped leaves (reserve the inner leaves for another use). Arrange on several serving platters.

Using 2 forks, mound about 2 tablespoons of the crab salad in each radicchio cup. Serve at once, or refrigerate for up to 1 hour. Let stand at room temperature for 10 minutes before serving.

MAKES 40 CUPS, OR 10–12 SERVINGS

1 fennel bulb, trimmed, quartered, cored, and coarsely chopped

1 lb lump Dungeness or other lump crabmeat, picked over for cartilage and shell fragments

2 shallots, very finely chopped

2 celery stalks, finely diced

2 tablespoons finely snipped fresh chives

2 tablespoons finely chopped fresh flat-leaf parsley

3 tablespoons white or black truffle oil

1½ tablespoons fresh lemon juice

1 tablespoon mayonnaise

Coarse salt and freshly ground pepper

3 large or 4 medium heads radicchio

Cremini Mushrooms Stuffed with Creamy Spinach and Quail Eggs

Steaming the mushrooms helps to rid them of excess moisture, creating a more concentrated mushroom flavor. They have a high moisture content, however, so they will shrink noticeably. For a photo of the recipe, see page 129.

Place the spinach in a colander and squeeze out as much moisture as possible. Transfer to a bowl and mix in the crème fraîche, Parmesan, and ½ teaspoon each salt and pepper.

Preheat oven to 400°F. Oil 2 baking dishes large enough to accommodate the mushrooms in a single layer. Put the mushroom caps, rounded side up, in a steamer basket set over simmering water. Cover and steam until tender and glossy, about 4 minutes. Lift out the basket and let drain.

Spoon about 1 tablespoon of the spinach mixture into each mushroom cap and smooth into a mound. With your pinky finger, make a shallow depression in the top of the stuffing to hold a quail egg. Place the mushrooms in the prepared dishes. Carefully break a quail egg into each depression and drizzle wine around the edges.

Bake until the eggs are set, 10–12 minutes. Let cool for 5 minutes, then dust each yolk with a pinch of paprika. Serve warm or at warm room temperature.

MAKES 40 MUSHROOMS, OR 10–12 SERVINGS

2 packages (10 oz each) frozen spinach, thawed

½ cup crème fraîche

⅓ cup grated Parmesan cheese

Salt and freshly ground pepper

40 fresh cremini or white button mushrooms, each 2–3 inches in diameter, brushed clean and stems removed

40 quail eggs

2 tablespoons dry white wine

Paprika, for garnish

Thyme-Roasted Short Ribs with Orange Gremolata

These meaty ribs are treated to a basting sauce made with richly colored Chinese dark soy sauce, sometimes labeled "superior" soy sauce, to which molasses has been added. If you can't find it, substitute 1 tablespoon honey and 3 tablespoons soy sauce. You can parboil these ribs the night before the party, cool to room temperature, cover, and refrigerate, then roast the next day.

6–6½ lb beef short ribs, cut into 2-inch lengths by the butcher

1 tablespoon red wine vinegar

1 tablespoon olive oil

3 cloves garlic, pressed or finely mashed in a mortar

⅓ cup fresh lemon juice

¼ cup sweet soy sauce

ORANGE GREMOLATA

Finely chopped zest of 2 oranges

3 tablespoons finely chopped garlic

3 tablespoons finely chopped fresh flat-leaf parsley

Place the ribs in a large saucepan and pour in cold water to cover. Add the vinegar, cover, and bring to a boil over high heat. Adjust the heat to a gentle simmer and cook, partially covered, for 8 minutes. Drain in a colander.

Preheat oven to 325°F. Place a large rack over a 12-by-17-inch rimmed baking sheet (or use 2 racks and 2 smaller rimmed baking sheets). Arrange the ribs, meaty side up, on the rack(s). Do not allow them to touch one another.

In a small saucepan over medium-low heat, warm the olive oil. Add the garlic and cook until completely tender, about 5 minutes. Stir in the lemon juice and sweet soy sauce and remove from the heat. Brush the ribs with some of the garlic-lemon mixture.

Slow-roast the ribs for 30 minutes, then baste with more garlic-lemon mixture and rotate a quarter-turn to one side. Baste again and roast for 30 minutes longer, then remove from oven. (At this point, you can let the ribs cool to room temperature, cover, and refrigerate for up to 6 hours. Bring to room temperature for 1 hour before continuing.) Raise oven temperature to 400°F. Arrange the ribs directly on the baking sheet(s) and roast until crisp and golden brown, about 15 minutes.

To make the *gremolata*, in a bowl, combine the orange zest, garlic, and parsley and mix with a fork until evenly blended. (The *gremolata* may be prepared up to 2 hours ahead; cover and refrigerate until serving.)

Transfer the ribs to platters and place a generous pinch of *gremolata* on top of each rib. Serve with napkins on the side.

MAKES 10–12 SERVINGS

Chard Fritters with Yogurt-Garlic-Chive Dipping Sauce

Infused with garlic and chives, this tasty sauce is best when made with full-fat or low-fat plain yogurt. Nonfat yogurt contains thickeners that yield an unnaturally glossy look. To speed up the frying process, use two pans, and perhaps enlist the help of one of your guests.

To make the yogurt sauce, in a bowl, combine the yogurt, garlic, chives, parsley, ½ teaspoon salt, and ¼ teaspoon white pepper and whisk to blend. Taste and adjust the seasoning. Cover and refrigerate for up to 6 hours before serving.

Bring a large pot three-fourths full of lightly salted water to a boil, add the chard leaves, and cook until wilted and dark, about 8 minutes. Drain in a colander under cold running water to stop the cooking. Squeeze the chard as dry as possible and chop coarsely. (The chard may be prepared up to this point, covered, and refrigerated for up to 6 hours before cooking the fritters.)

In a large bowl, combine the flour, polenta or cornmeal, milk, and egg yolks. Stir together with a sturdy rubber spatula until smooth. The mixture will be very thick. Cover and let stand at room temperature for 30 minutes.

Add the chard, parsley, 1 teaspoon salt, and a little black pepper to the fritter batter. Blend thoroughly with a fork.

Preheat oven to 150°F. Line a baking sheet with paper towels. Place a very large, heavy frying pan (preferably cast iron) over medium-high heat and pour in olive oil to a depth of ⅛ inch. Working in batches, scoop up 1 tablespoon batter for each fritter and slip it into the hot oil; be careful not to crowd the pan. Fry the fritters, turning once, until golden brown on both sides, 1–1½ minutes on each side. Adjust the heat so the fritters brown and sizzle but do not burn. As each batch is done, use a slotted spoon to transfer the fritters to the prepared baking sheet. Place more paper towels on the top and press gently to blot up any excess oil.

You can keep the fritters warm in the oven for up to 10 minutes before serving. Arrange them on platters and serve the cold yogurt sauce alongside.

MAKES ABOUT 40 FRITTERS, OR 10–12 SERVINGS

YOGURT SAUCE

1½ cups plain yogurt (see note)

3 cloves garlic, minced or pressed

3 tablespoons finely snipped fresh chives

1½ tablespoons finely chopped fresh flat-leaf parsley

Coarse salt and freshly ground white pepper

CHARD FRITTERS

½ lb Swiss chard leaves, thick stems removed

2¾ cups all-purpose flour

½ cup polenta or coarse-grind cornmeal

1½ cups whole milk

5 large egg yolks, lightly beaten

¼ cup finely chopped fresh flat-leaf parsley

Coarse salt and freshly ground black pepper

Olive oil, for frying

Polenta Crostini Topped with Smoked Trout, Apple, and Walnut Salad

Golden squares of polenta, flavored with Parmesan, are the perfect vehicle for this smoked trout salad. For even more color, brush the polenta squares with melted butter and slip them under a hot broiler until crisp and golden brown, about 5 minutes, then let cool before topping.

In a large, heavy saucepan, cook the polenta according to package instructions. Vigorously stir in the butter and Parmesan until evenly distributed. Remove from the heat. Quickly rinse a 12-by-17-inch rimmed baking sheet with cold water and shake it dry. Immediately mound the polenta in the pan and, working quickly and using a spatula repeatedly dipped in hot water, spread the polenta in an even layer about ½ inch thick. Cover with a kitchen towel and let stand for at least 1 hour at room temperature or refrigerate for up to 24 hours. Bring the chilled polenta to room temperature for about 1 hour before serving. Cut the polenta into 2-inch squares and arrange on platters.

To make the salad, in a bowl, combine the trout, apples, walnuts, ¼ cup mayonnaise, lemon juice, ¼ teaspoon salt, and pepper to taste. Stir with a fork until evenly blended. (It should clump slightly; if necessary, add more mayonnaise.) Mound 1 tablespoon on each polenta square and scatter with chives and a grind of pepper. Serve within 30 minutes.

MAKES 10–12 SERVINGS

2 cups instant polenta

4 tablespoons unsalted butter

⅔ cup grated Parmesan cheese

SALAD

½ lb smoked trout, skin and bones removed, finely chopped

2 small Gala or Fuji apples, peeled, cored, and finely diced

¾ cup coarsely chopped walnuts

¼ cup mayonnaise, plus more if needed

1 tablespoon fresh lemon juice

Coarse salt and freshly ground pepper

2 tablespoons finely snipped fresh chives

Belgian Endive Spears Topped with Goat Cheese and Chopped Pistachios

Look for Belgian endives with tightly furled leaves ending in white or pale yellow tips. For a festive presentation, use ½ teaspoon salmon roe in place of the nut garnish on half of the spears. For a photo of the recipe, see page 129.

In a bowl, beat together the goat cheese and cream with a fork until fluffy. Set aside. If the pistachios have remnants of skin still attached, rub them gently in a kitchen towel. Transfer the cleaned nuts to a cutting board and chop finely.

Trim the endive ends and carefully separate the leaves without breaking. As the leaves get smaller, trim the base a little more. Choose 40 of the largest, most perfect spears (reserve the smaller spears for salad). Arrange on platters, with the pointed ends outward.

Using a fork and spoon, mound 2 teaspoons of the goat cheese mixture onto the blunt end of each spear, smearing it a little to help it adhere. Scatter 1 teaspoon of the nuts over the goat cheese on each spear, pressing them gently into the cheese. Let stand at room temperature for up to 30 minutes, or refrigerate for up to 2 hours, before serving.

MAKES ABOUT 40 SPEARS, OR 10–12 SERVINGS

¾ lb mild fresh goat cheese such as Montrachet, at room temperature

¼ cup heavy cream

¾ cup unsalted pistachio nuts

5 large, firm heads Belgian endive

Lemon-Lime Tartlets

You will need nonstick muffin pans with miniature cups—1⅞ inches in diameter and ¾ inch deep—for making these bite-sized sunny yellow tartlets. Most of these miniature pans, also known as gem pans, have 12 or 24 cups.

PASTRY

1¾ cups plus 1 tablespoon all-purpose flour

Pinch of sea salt

½ cup plus 1 tablespoon very cold unsalted butter, cut into small cubes

3–4 tablespoons water

2–3 tablespoons fresh orange juice

FILLING

3 large whole eggs, plus 3 large egg yolks

Grated zest of 1 lemon, plus more for garnish

½ cup fresh lemon juice

¼ cup fresh lime juice

⅓ cup water

½ cup sugar

4 tablespoons unsalted butter, cut into 4 equal pieces

Grated zest of 1 lime

To make the pastry, in a food processor, combine the flour and salt and pulse to mix. Add the butter and pulse 4 or 5 times in 2-second bursts, or until the mixture resembles large bread crumbs. Remove the cover and drizzle 3 tablespoons water and 2 tablespoons orange juice evenly over the mixture. Pulse again just until the dough forms a rough, shaggy mass on the center stem. If the dough does not come together within 5–10 seconds, sprinkle with up to 1 additional tablespoon each water and orange juice in 2-teaspoon increments until it does; do not overwork. Turn out onto a lightly floured work surface, form into a ball, and then flatten into a disk 2 inches thick. Wrap with plastic wrap and refrigerate for at least 3 hours or up to overnight.

On a lightly floured work surface, roll out the dough ⅛ inch thick. Using a 2½-inch round cookie cutter, cut out as many dough rounds as possible; you should have 32–36. Gently press each dough round into the cup of a nonstick mini-muffin pan, easing the dough up the sides. Refrigerate for at least 20 minutes or up to 4 hours before baking.

Meanwhile, make the filling. In a bowl, beat together the whole eggs and egg yolks until blended; set aside. In the top of a double boiler set over (but not touching) barely simmering water, combine the lemon zest, lemon juice, lime juice, water, sugar, and butter and stir until the sugar is dissolved and the butter is melted. Remove from the heat and let cool for 5 minutes. Working in ¼-cup batches, whisk the lemon mixture into the beaten eggs, then return the egg-lemon mixture to the top of the double boiler. Cook over low heat, stirring frequently but not constantly, until the mixture is very thick, about 15 minutes. Strain through a fine-mesh sieve into a bowl. (The filling can be prepared up to this point, covered, and refrigerated for up to 4 hours before assembling the tarts.)

Preheat oven to 400°F. Cut out 3-inch rounds of parchment paper, place one in each tartlet shell, and fill with pie weights or raw rice to ensure that the tartlet shells hold their shape during baking.

Bake the tartlet shells until the edges are golden, 10–15 minutes. Let cool in the pans on a wire rack for 10 minutes; reduce oven temperature to 375°F. Remove the pie weights and parchment rounds. Spoon about 1 tablespoon of the filling into each tartlet shell. Return the tartlets to oven and bake until the filling is set but not browned, about 10 minutes. Let cool completely on the wire rack.

Serve at room temperature or refrigerate for up to 2 hours and serve chilled. Scatter a pinch each of lime and lemon zest over each tartlet just before serving.

MAKES 32–36 TARTLETS, OR 10–12 SERVINGS

Fallen Chocolate Cake with Chocolate Shavings

This flourless cake, or torte, is slightly undercooked, which yields a fudgy center reminiscent of chocolate mousse. The gold leaf, a traditional decoration for sweet and savory celebratory Indian dishes, can be found in specialty baking stores and Indian groceries.

Preheat oven to 375°F. Generously grease a 10-inch springform or round cake pan. Cut out a round of parchment paper to fit the bottom. Fit it in the pan, pressing until smooth. Generously grease the paper and pan sides, then dust the paper and pan sides thoroughly with cocoa powder and tap out any excess. Place the pan on a baking sheet.

In a large, stainless-steel bowl set over (but not touching) simmering water, melt the butter with the chocolate, stirring once or twice, until smooth, 5–7 minutes. Remove from the heat and set aside.

In a bowl, using a stand mixer fitted with the whip attachment or a handheld mixer, beat together the whole eggs, egg yolk, salt, and sugar on high speed until the volume nearly triples and the mixture is almost white, 5–10 minutes. To test if it is ready, lift a little of the mixture with the beater; it should fall back into the bowl and form a slowly dissolving ribbon on the surface. Add the egg mixture and the ground almonds to the melted chocolate mixture, then sift the cornstarch over the top. Using a rubber spatula, gently fold together until smooth and evenly blended; do not overmix. Pour the batter into the prepared pan. (The batter can be prepared up to this point, covered with plastic wrap, and refrigerated for up to 8 hours. Bring to room temperature for 15 minutes before baking.)

Bake the cake until it puffs and is slightly crusty and the center jiggles a little when the pan is shaken, 25–27 minutes. Let cool in the pan for 15 minutes (or leave in the pan for up to 45 minutes before serving, to keep warm).

While the cake is baking, make the shavings: In the top of a double boiler set over (but not touching) simmering water, melt the chocolate, stirring constantly, until smooth. Pour the melted chocolate over an inverted baking sheet and spread to a thin and even coat with a thin, metal spatula. Chill the pan until the chocolate has hardened, at least 10 minutes. Let the chocolate stand at room temperature for 5 minutes, then scrape it away from the pan with the back of the spatula, forming curls.

Run a thin knife around the inside edge of the pan to loosen the cake. Place a platter upside down over the pan, invert the pan and platter together, lift off the pan, and peel off the parchment. Dust the cake generously with cocoa. Using wooden skewers, carefully transfer the shavings to the cake. If using the gold leaf, use a small, dry paintbrush to remove it from its paper and apply it to the chocolate shavings. Serve warm or at warm room temperature, cut into very thin slices.

MAKES 10–12 SERVINGS

Unsweetened cocoa powder, for dusting pan and finished cake

⅔ cup unsalted butter, at room temperature

9 oz bittersweet or semisweet chocolate, coarsely chopped

5 large whole eggs, plus 1 large egg yolk

¼ teaspoon salt

⅔ cup sugar

¼ cup ground almonds

2 teaspoons cornstarch

CHOCOLATE SHAVINGS

4 oz bittersweet chocolate, coarsely chopped

Edible gold leaf (optional)

INDEX